Coping with the 21st Century

PETER COREY

Illustrated by
Mike Phillips

Scholastic Children's Books
Commonwealth House, 1–19 New Oxford Street
London WC1A 1NU, UK

A division of Scholastic Ltd
London ~ New York ~ Toronto ~ Sydney ~ Auckland
Mexico City ~ New Delhi ~ Hong Kong

First published by Scholastic Ltd, 1999

ISBN 0 590 11192 2

Typeset by TW Typesetting, Midsomer Norton, Somerset

Printed by Cox & Wyman Ltd, Reading, Berks.

10 9 8 7 6 5 4 3 2 1

Contents

Dedication:

This book is dedicated to everyone who has made it this far. How are you going to feel when you realize that although you're still really young your life spans two millennia?

Author's Note:

At the very moment that this book first hit the shops and book clubs, the entire world was in the grip of pre-Millennium fever.

However, you may be reading it a couple of years later. You may even be reading it 20 years later, by which time it will undoubtedly be a set text in the new Smartypants exam that is destined to replace GCSEs. You may even have dug it up from a retrieval system, as a perfect example of the sort of thing that inspired the human race in the dying days of the 20th century. In any of the above scenarios you will instantly realize that the book is written from a 1999 perspective. And if you don't, then let me point out straight away that it is. Because of this you may find that some of the things predicted in this book have already happened. In which case let me take this opportunity to say "I told you so!"

The 21st Century – so what?

It is 31 December 1999, and as people throughout the land cross their arms and link hands to sing "Auld Lang Syne" – wondering who the person next to them is and what the heck the words mean – more than a few of them will be wondering what is so special about the year 2000. OK, so you'll get into trouble for a few weeks for putting the wrong date on your school work, but that happens every year, doesn't it? It's hardly life threatening, is it?

Computers might be another matter. Thousands of them worldwide will crash because the various people who run them ignored the warnings about computers not being able to cope with a change of century. You can hardly blame the computers, can you? After all, they're not built to last. The technology goes out of date as soon as it's installed. How were they supposed to know that they'd be around in the next century, even if it is only a few months away?

But the effect of this could be far-reaching. People who get paid by computer might not get their dosh. Patients whose hospital appointments are sent to them by computer might never get that life-saving, or life-threatening, operation. Worse still they might go into hospital for a tonsillectomy, and wind up having a leg off.

But if you haven't got a job or dodgy tonsils this is not going to affect you, is it? So just what is all the fuss about? Why is the 21st century going to be so hard to cope with? And obviously it *is* going to be hard to cope with otherwise I would not be writing this book. I'll tell you: The reason the 21st century is going to be hard to cope with is because it's really, really important.

In what way?

Simply because it *is* a new century. It'll be seen as a new beginning; a great opportunity for *new stuff* to happen; a chance to *improve* on anything that our ancestors did, because it's all part of human nature to try and be better than the previous generation[1].

"But what makes the 21st century any worse than, say, the 20th century?" I hear you cry.

I'll tell you anyway – whether you're crying or not. It will be much, much harder to cope with for the simple reason that not only is it the start of a new century, but it's also the start of a new *millennium*.

A new what?

A new millennium – what is it?

The good old *Cambridge Pocket Dictionary*, which as you know is the size of two adult African elephants bound together with parcel tape, tells us – and I quote – that a *millennium* is:

1. In the case of parents, of course, this is almost too easy.

1. A span of one thousand years.
2. A hoped-for period of joy, serenity, prosperity and justice.
3 A thousandth anniversary.
This is based on the Latin *mille* meaning thousand, and *annus* meaning year. This is not to be confused with *milli* meaning *million*, or *anus* meaning bottom, in which case *millennium* would mean "a million bottoms".

Now I don't know about you - in fact, I've probably never even *met* you - but I find this a bit confusing. Why is a thousand years called a *millennium?* Why isn't it a million years? To try and find out I did a bit of checking and apparently the word *million* is Middle English, coming from the Old French *milion*, which in turn comes from the Old Italian *milione*, which comes from ... yes! You've guessed it! The Latin *mille*.

Which does absolutely nothing to help explain why a millennium is a thousand years and not a million. By rights a millennium should be a million years, and a thousand-year period should be called a thoussusium or something. Not that the Powers That Be - Romans probably - gave a monkey's about how long a millennium was. They were too busy taking over the known world, and covering it in roads and plumbing.

If it didn't move they conquered it, and if it *did* move they fed it to the lions. But they were no different from anybody else, where time was concerned.

It's a funny thing, time

How do you think your average dinosaur would react to you telling it that, even though it lived 500 million years ago, we were still only on the threshold of the third millennium? It'd bite your head off probably. That is until you pointed out that you were talking about AD.

AD – what's that then? It stands for *anno Domini* – not *After Dinner* – and means "in the year of the Lord". So AD 1 was the date set for the birth of Christ. None of which explains why a *millennium* is so called, but still. I suppose having finally agreed on a start date for time, arguing the toss about what to call a thousand-year period was not even on the agenda. After all, it wasn't going to affect anybody involved in the beginning-of-time calculation was it, because by the time the first millennium came along they would be long gone.

Of course, this start date for time only applies to Christians. Other religions have their own time scales; as far as Jewish people are concerned, for example, the year 2000 is actually the year 5760. And just to make things more complicated, the Islamic calendar makes it 2622, and the Chinese calendar makes it the Year of the Rabbit[1]. At least January and February are anyway. The rest of the year is the Year of the Dragon.

Confused? You should be. But it could be worse. After all, if everyone was working to their own time-scale letters would arrive hundred of years before they were posted, instead of hundreds of years afterwards which is the current system. Fortunately, everyone has agreed to work to the same time-scale and therefore we find ourselves on the threshold of a new millennium.

A time of new beginnings.

1. Or the Cat, depending on which books you read!

A *significant* time.

To understand why it's so significant we need to understand the traditional meaning of the year.

The circle of life

No, this is not a song from a Disney classic. Well, it is actually, but that's not what I'm talking about. Traditionally the year represented the circle of life. The year began in about March/April with the planting of new seeds, although they weren't called March and April in those days. Oh – and the year only had ten months. At least, it did until the Romans got their hands on it. They renamed all the months, and added a couple more just to show off. But whether you followed the Roman year or the Saxon one, the beginning of each New Year was very, very important. It symbolized a new beginning: new crops, new animals, new battles. It was also a great excuse for a party, as it is today.

And here I think we're getting closer to what the millennium is all about. After all, if New Year is the perfect excuse to eat and drink too much and dance around to obscure Scottish songs, what is the celebration for the beginning of a new century going to be like? A hundred times bigger, probably. And if celebrating the beginning of a new century is a great excuse to push the boat out, celebrating a new millennium must be a great excuse to go on a world cruise. Figuratively speaking. Have a huge great party, anyway. And that's what it's about. Party time. Dressed up as a significant New Beginning.

You don't believe me? In which case let's slip back to AD 999.

Dial AD 999

It's significant that something that was described at the time as the

and

should have happened in the dying days of the year 999, because apparently if the police hadn't been called it might still be going on! So how did it come about?

To find out we need to turn to the crumbled pages of "*Fyluf Fiff*bury'*f* Big Book of *f*tuff", one of the most learned chronicles of the late 10th century. In it *Fyluf fetf* the *f*cene – sorry, I mean Sylus sets the scene:

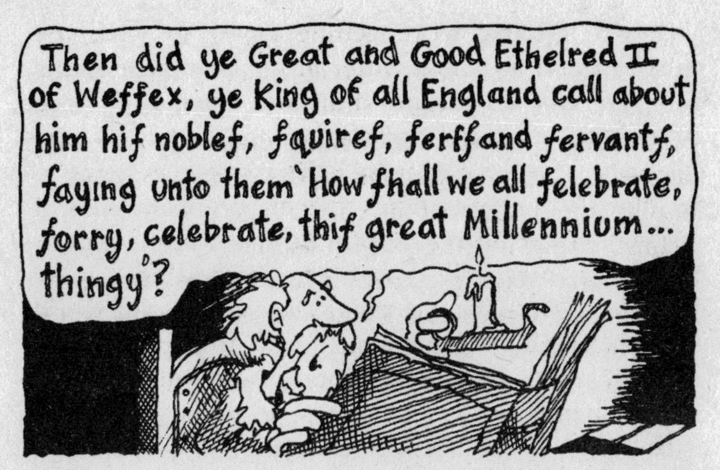

Good queftion, sorry, question. After all, what was there to celebrate? The 10th century was hardly the age of discovery[1]. Oh yes, the Chinese had discovered printing, and the Vikings had discovered that if you hit anyone over the head for long enough they would give you their lands, but that was about it. But did this put Ethelred II off? Not at all. He ordered that

and, according to Sylus Sissbury,

1. Not in the West, anyway.

Naturally there was a great outcry. Most people couldn't see why they should be bothering with celebrating the New Millennium, especially when the taxpayer – i.e. the peasant in the street – would be footing the bill. Most of them hadn't got two half-pennies to rub together, which was hardly surprising, as halfpennies hadn't been invented then. Soon the peasants were revolting. There were no newspapers to write to and complain, but if you bought the local ballad singer a pint of Ye Olde Futtuck's Mead he'd sing a song along the lines of: "Keep your hands off our lovely green fields and take your disgusting millennium construction elsewhere or I'll set my dog on to you (repeat chorus three times)", etc., to a tune vaguely resembling something by the Levellers.

Soon, the anti-Millennium feeling was so great the people started to get ill over it; the disease was called *millennium doom*. What was Ethelred to do? He had a brainwave. After all he was a great king. Not as great as Alfred, who after all was so great that he was even known as Alfred the Great, even if he was lousy at cooking. Ethelred got around the problem of the revolting peasants by announcing that:

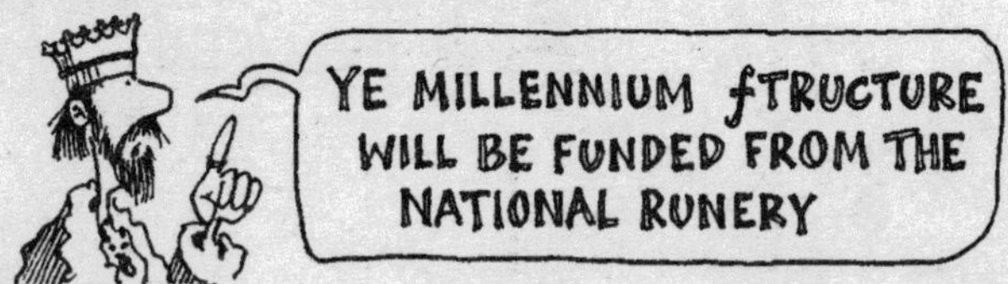

The National Runery had been another of Ethelred's "Big Idea*ſ*", when his royal advisors told him that he had better not increase taxes again – "not unle*ſſ* thou think*ſt* that thou would*ſt* enjoy having part*ſ* of thy body removed with ye ru*ſt*y old *ſ*oup *ſ*poon, my liege."

The National Runery was a brainwave, even if it was

a complicated business. This is how it worked:

Anyone wishing to take part would write, or get someone who could actually write to write, their six runes on a piece of parchment, attach the parchment to a large bag of gold, then attach both things to a carrier pigeon (a pretty big pigeon, naturally) and send the whole lot to Runery Headquarters, at Camelot, not surprisingly, to arrive no later than "Ye hour at which ye cock doth crow on ye morn of Saturn's Day" i.e. very early on a Saturday morning.

The winner(s) would then be announced by the official National Runery Ballad Singer, some time in the next fifty years. The reason for the delay was because there were only two official National Runery Ballad Singers and England was a large and dangerous place, even then.

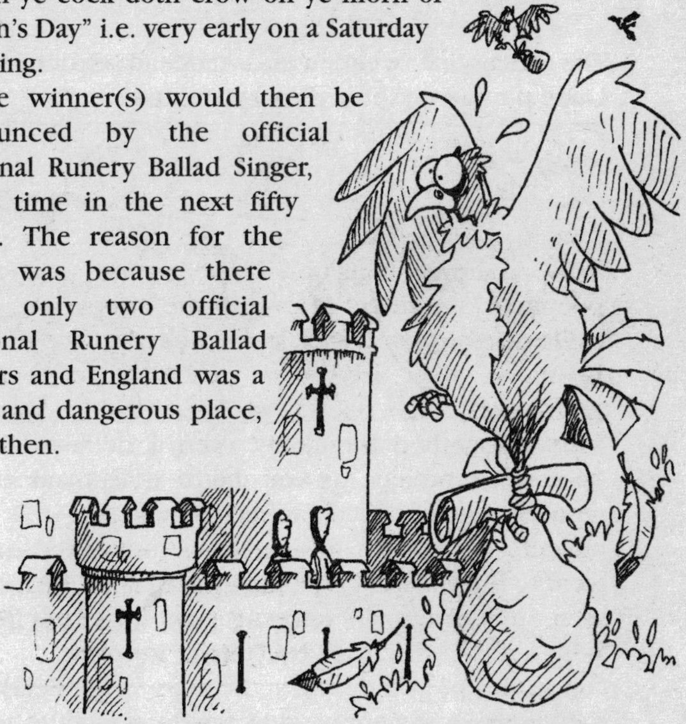

The prize each week varied to keep it interesting. One week it would be a couple of chickens, and next it would be the death penalty. They never gave money away, arguing that there would be no point in asking people to part with their hard-earned cash to take part in the Runery, if they were then going to get a chance to win it back, albeit a very slim chance. For those of you who are fascinated by such details, the winning runes on the first ever National Runery (presented by Winton A'Dale) were

♐ ⊿ ♌ ♓ ♑ ♈

and the bonus rune was

♎

The prize that week was a medium-sized haddock. Quite popular in those days apparently.

By this method the money was quickly raised for the Millennium project, as you might well imagine. And tenders to build it were invited. That is to say that three builders were asked to name their price, and the job went to the cheapest one. But – as anyone who has ever seen Stonehenge will know – it never got completed. Why not? Because they tried to do it on the cheap, or "on ye cheap" as they said at the time. You see, although they wanted something that would stand the test of time, the general feeling was that in an age when the life span of your average peasant was about twenty minutes there wasn't a lot of point in splashing out too much cash on it. Originally a Clayhenge was built, but unfortunately it only lasted a day because it rained.

Then some bright spark suggested a Glasshenge, made of clear glass. There were only really two things against this idea:

a) Nobody would be able to see it.

b) It would take ages to clean. And...

c) Clear glass wasn't really available in Britain. You could send abroad for it, but it always got broken in the post.

Sorry - three things.

Then a Bonehenge was started, but a pack of dogs ran off with it.

Finally, huge stones were rolled all the way from Wales, and erected. Unfortunately the money ran out before the thing was completed, there was a huge row about the bill, and there it stands to this day[1]. Obviously the party went ahead, because it seemed a shame to waste the food.

Trainspotters may wish to know that the menu that day included "Glaſtonbury Abbey White Wine: Trod by ye monkſ themſelves, which do give ye wine a diſtinctive taſte of leather ſandleſ and veruccaſ" and "Aſſorted canapeſ". This turned out be "assorted canned apes", the most popular (i.e. least disgusting) of which was "monkey in a mushroom sauce".

1. Well, it's a theory, anyway! In fact, my research tells me that Stonehenge was built in 2000 BC - presumably to celebrate a much earlier millennium.

The entertainment included jugglers and a couple of Celts being burned at the stake. It was just the sort of bash that Ethelred enjoyed.

The point is that if they were prepared to throw a party on this kind of scale, plus attempt to build something as huge and completely pointless as Stonehenge to celebrate the Millennium at a time when half of the known world was mud and the most exciting thing that could happen to you was to get your large intestine pulled out via your left nostril by a marauding Viking (and only then if you were *really* lucky), then what are they likely to do *now*? And *why*?

Then and now

As they stood around at the first millennium celebrations in the husk of a half-finished henge, nibbling barbecued boar's buttocks and muttering about never knowing whether the henge would look great when it was finished or not, were they thinking ahead to what the next thousand years held, or were they reflecting on past glories?

Certainly the king might have been reflecting on his own personal success. For one thing he'd hung on to his crown for 21 years, which was no mean feat when most of his predecessors hadn't lasted more than about four. But he hadn't made a huge difference culturally.

Culture had largely been left to other people. China, for instance, had invented printing and had more letters in its alphabet than you could possibly need even if you were writing to your mother; Rome had conquered most of the world and introduced it to the mysteries of Italian ice-cream.

And then there was Egypt. The ancient Egyptians had developed more cultural ideas and invented more stuff than you could wave a pointy stick at[1].

Take shaving, for example. The Egyptians were keen shavers. But being an incredibly advanced civilization they had to have the right equipment. No scraping your sword around your chops and hoping you didn't cut your head off for them, oh no! After much experimentation, most of it involving Moses and the Children of Israel[2], some bright spark invented a tiny blade which, being razor-sharp, he called a *razor blade*. But how to keep it sharp – that was the puzzle. The same bright spark discovered that if you built a huge pyramid shape out of stone and hung your used razor blade inside it, by the morning it was sharp again. This was discovered by more careful experimentation. Bright Spark – we'll call him Eric – tried various methods; he hung his razor upside down inside an old shoe box, stuffed it down the back of his trousers and hung it from the end of a high

1. And waving a pointy stick was pretty popular in those days.
2. Which explains why some of them never grew up to be the Adults of Israel.

priest's[1] nose, but oddly enough none of these methods worked[2].

The pyramid razor-blade sharpener became so popular that the Egyptian royal family all had themselves buried inside one, so that they need never worry about accidentally growing a beard, even in death. They also wrapped themselves in bandages in case they cut themselves shaving.

Because of his discovery Eric the Egyptian became a wealthy and popular man. Not all of his inventions were such a success, however. His cuddly toy, pictured here, was a complete disaster, mainly because it was a bit big and made out of stone.

But this kind of initiative would have left the likes of Ethelred II totally breathless. He wouldn't even know where to begin. Unfortunately many of ancient Egypt's cultural breakthroughs were lost. Apparently they had a huge millennium party to celebrate their cultural genius. It was so riotous and went on so long, that in the morning they'd forgotten almost everything they'd ever

1. How high? Six feet.

2. Strangely the one place he didn't hang it was directly above a knife sharpener's grinding wheel, but then the ancient Egyptians were never ones to go for the easy option.

invented. Hence another hugely advanced civilization bit the dust, and all on account of too much crocodile lager.

None of this concerned Ethelred II as he gazed out across Salisbury, where on the distant horizon, the sky glowed red.

"Red ſky at night ſhepherdſ delight..." he probably started saying to himself, although he might not have done. But if he had he would have been wrong. This was no good omen for local shepherds; it was just the local Danes putting yet another unsuspecting village to the torch.

If Ethelred and his fellow Saxons had little or nothing to reflect on as they stood on the threshold of their millennium celebrations in 999, were they looking ahead to the future much as we are now? An informed educated answer would be "probably", although whether they had the slightest notion what the next thousand years would hold is another matter. If, for instance, they'd known that in 67 years' time they'd be Normans and not Saxons, eating frogs' legs and living in cul-de-sacs, that might have thrown a whole new light on things. But they didn't. Any more than we know what the next thousand years holds.

Lack of faith in the future

There was one group at that 999 millennium celebration that knew exactly what was going to happen – or thought they did. They stood, smug, a few hundred metres from the main crowd, just inside the rope cordon that was holding back the hordes of Japanese sightseers, waving their banners in a resigned manner, and waiting. To the casual observer they were just a bunch of loonies in long white nighties with paper hats and strange symbols painted on their faces. But to anyone "in the know" (i.e. almost nobody) they were The Children of the Wooden Persuasion, with their leader Gamma Pasternak (Ms).

The Children of the Wooden Persuasion were a religious splinter group. Whilst the rest of Britain were prepared to believe in One God who made man in His own image, except on Thursday when they worshipped Thor, The Children of the Wooden Persuasion had but

one belief: that "On ye ſtroke on ye midnite on ye laſt day in ye year of our Lord 999, ye worlde will be conſumed in a burning fire, and ye Lord our God will wreak hiſ terrible almighty vengeance on uſ, hiſ ſinful ſubjectſ. ſo there!"

In other words, the world was going to come to an end. As everyone else charged their glasses, or rather pewter mugs, The Children of the Wooden Persuasion prepared to be engulfed in fire prior to meeting their Maker; though why they should imagine that God would be the least bit interested in meeting a bunch of characters who looked like they'd just jumped off a barbecue rather too late, is beyond me. And didn't they all look pretty silly – sorry, sill*ier* – when at midnight everyone else linked arms and sang "Auld Lang Syne" and the world didn't end.

There would have been much checking of timepieces and charts, and then it would have been a case of all back to Gamma's place for a regroup. She'd probably have to offer to snog them all, just to keep the group together.

In the run-up to midnight Ethelred would have been trying to decide what to do about them. After all, they were real party poopers, particularly with those banners which said things like "*We're all going to die in about ten minutes and there's naff-all we can do about it*" (or words to that effect) and "*Frying tonight*". That's just the sort of stuff that wrecks even the best-organized party. It even works faster than sticking on an All Saints record.

Ethelred would have contemplated having Ms Pasternak burned as a witch, but witch-burning wasn't really as popular then as it later became. In 999 the official line on witches was to ignore them and they'd go away; sometimes not until they'd turned you into a toad, but that was the risk you took.

Ethelred already had a slightly toad-like appearance which had done him no favours in the "love department", and so he chose to ignore them. Quite wisely as it turned out. Twenty minutes later *The Children of the Wooden Persuasion* were shambling off, muttering things like "we could try again next Tuesday", whilst Ethelred and his subjects pointed and laughed.

What Ethelred and the others would not have realized is that millions of people shared Ms Pasternak's fears. It was a condition known as *End-of-the-millennium psychosis*.

End-of-the-millennium what?!?

End-of-the-millennium psychosis. A strong belief that the world would end at the beginning of a new millennium. Of course, believing that the world would end is not new. Nostradamus, the 16th-century French astrologer and clever clogs predicted that the world would end in the year 2000, after a huge war in 1999.

Cheerful chap, wasn't he? Actually, all he was doing was reflecting thinking of the time. Many people believed that the world would not survive past the end of the millennium. Not that any of them would be there to see it, but it still bothered them.

Even the *Sun* newspaper has reported the end of the world. It is going to happen, apparently, on Thursday 26 October 2028, at 5.30 pm, just as you're sitting down for your tea. What will happen is a huge meteorite will collide with the Earth at a speed of 17,000 m.p.h., causing an explosion equal to 320,000 megatons of dynamite and leaving a crater a mile wide, and a shocked expression on the face of anyone unlucky enough to be standing in the way. Alternatively it might miss by 26,000 miles. Either way I suggest you don't do your homework until after tea on that day; after all it could be a waste of effort!

However, assuming that the prophecies are wrong, we will be standing on New Year's Eve 1999, much as Ethelred did in 999, and wondering what the future holds.

Looking ahead- agh! Watch Out!

Of course, unlike Ethelred and his lot, we are in a position to make informed guesses about what the future might hold[1]. How? By studying previous historic events and developments. History does have a sort of logic to it, and by studying this logic we should be able to predict some of the events for the next millennium. Maybe. If we're lucky. It's worth a try.

Broken bottles in the sands of time

You would be amazed how much past events affect our lives today. For example: the Danes invaded the Isle of Wight in 998 (this was probably still being talked about at the millennium celebrations of 999). Now, if you go to the Isle of Wight today, you can get a very nice Danish pastry in a little shop in Ventnor[2]. Of course, these two events may not be linked in any way, but I rather think that the recipe for those Danish pastries was left behind by some marauding Dane. This begs the question: if the Danes had never invaded, what would the Danish pastries on the Isle of Wight taste like? Would they even exist?

And what about everything else? How do the discoveries of the past affect the future? Take money, for instance; way back in...

1. Not to mention what the future might try and hold, but drop because it's so squelchy and slippy that you can't really get a decent grip on it.
2. On the Isle of Wight, obviously!

2000 BC The first metal "coins" appeared. Before then cows had been used as currency. But because the price of everything was rounded up to the nearest cow, people realized they were being overcharged. These first coins were actually shaped like cows[1]. It's true[2]!

600 BC The first non-cow shaped coins were minted in Lydia in Asia Minor, and in China.

Money caught on as people from different countries started to move around and trade with each other. The Romans introduced a single currency for their expanding empire. And then in the 9th century China issued the first paper money. This didn't catch on for some time elsewhere; coins were the thing. By the Middle Ages they were so popular that people started minting their own. Any king, nobleman, or even wealthy merchant could have their head (or any other part of their body for that matter) stamped on their very own coins.

This obviously made things very confusing. By the time of the Norman Conquest there were 70 different lots of coins in England alone! In fact it was in this second millennium (1000–1999) that things really started to hot up, and many of the things we have now started coming into being. And of course it's these things that will affect our future.

From AD **1223**, when gold was first mined commercially, things really started to get going. Banks were set

1. The term "pecuniary", referring to money matters, comes from the Latin *pecus* meaning cattle.
2. OK, so the bit about rounding up to the nearest cow isn't – but the rest is!

up, paper money was used, traveller's cheques were invented (by American Express), credit cards were introduced, decimal currency, store cards, on and on right through to electronic banking and TV shopping! That's a huge change from using cows as currency! OK, so it's taken nearly 4,000 years, but it's still a huge change. And money is just the tip of the iceberg. What about...

Transport

Transport is a complex matter these days. Just getting to school on the bus can be a nightmare! But how did they cope way back in ancient times? For instance, in...

c. 3500 BC When the Sumerians in Mesopotamia invented the wheel, do you think they had the foggiest idea what they were starting? Do you think they even knew what they were trying to invent? Maybe it was going to be the very first personal hi-fi system, but not having the Japanese know-how, they couldn't make it small enough. It's not impossible. After all, Sir Walter Raleigh was obviously trying to invent the edible bowling bowl when he discovered the potato, just as AG Bell was trying to invent the Walkman when he came up with the telephone.

Well, whatever weird and wonderful plans the Sumerians had up their sleeves, they wound up with the wheel. And it was because of this that in...

c. 1668 BC The first horse[1]-drawn chariots arrived in Egypt, driven by invading Semites. The Egyptians had never seen a horse, and it's probably due to the fact that they were standing around pointing and saying things like: "Look at the size of that cat![2]" that they were overwhelmed by the invaders, who ruled Egypt for the next two centuries. Following this event, horses (and wheels) became the major means of transport for many centuries to come. All throughout the first millennium in fact. But when we get to...

The second millennium

Things start to change. For one thing people started to say "These wheels are really boring! (Or wheelie boring!) There's got to be another way to get around." And there was. There were the seas and rivers for a start. Various civilizations started hollowing out trees to make boats; or stretching animal skins over wooden frames - having removed and eaten the animal first of course - to make simple canoes. But did they stop there? Of course they didn't! And in...

1094 The first gondolas appeared in Venice. Made of wood quite probably. Oh yes - you can lead a horse to water, but you can't make a boat out of one; not a live one anyway. But horses were still a handy way of getting about, and in...

1519 Spanish explorer Hernando Cortez transported horses to America. Up until then they'd been getting around on piggyback, or buffalo. Boats at this point were still largely made of wood and driven by wind,

1. I'm not sure who invented the horse.
2. Ancient Egyptians, as you know, were very fond of cats.

until about…

1775 The first steam-powered boat was developed. Now I don't know how much you know about steam, but in order to make enough to drive a large boat you need either a very large electric kettle, or a big fire. And boats were made of wood. So naturally you can imagine that there was the occasional accident.

But did this put people off? No! And, having conquered the seas, they began to look skywards.

1783 First steam – then hot air! Joseph Michel and Jacques Etienne Montgolfier (what do you reckon they were, then – Welshmen?) became the first men to fly. No, they didn't eat tons of birdseed and jump off the roof, they built a hot-air balloon. They got the idea from watching wood chips float up from a burning fire. They realized that if they set fire to themselves, they too would go up in the air. No they didn't! They realized that hot air caused things to fly. They demonstrated their balloon to King Louis XVI, before he got his head chopped off, obviously. The King was impressed, and said: "Great balloon! But can you model it into the shape of a poodle?[1]". Not only did they fly themselves, but Michel and Montgolfier also carried a duck, a sheep and a cockerel, making them the first Frenchmen to transport livestock. And nobody protested.

1. Louis had seen some pretty fine children's entertainers in his time.

1804 By now inventors were moving well beyond balloons full of ducks, and James Trevithick invented the first steam locomotive. And in...

1863 The first underground railway opened in London. But public transport was all very well if you wanted to go to the same place as everybody else, but what if you wanted to go off on your own? Karl Benz realized this, and in...

1885 He developed the first petrol-driven motor car. It had three wheels. Not all along one side, I imagine. Meanwhile back in the skies, in...

1903 Wilbur and Orville Wright invented and tested the very first practical aeroplane. The first flight lasted 12 seconds, not quite long enough for the stewardess to complete the safety drill demonstration.

Within a few years aeroplanes were crossing the channel and fighting in the First World War.

1908 Car travel for all became a real possibility when Henry Ford developed the first cheap mass-produced

car, the Model T. Whatever happened to the Model A, B, C, D, etc.?
1912 Metal ships were now two a penny, although they cost a small fortune. You see, by now people had realized that although metal was very heavy, it wouldn't necessarily sink. Then the SS *Titanic*, one of the largest liners ever built, sank. Travel by ship had been popular for many years, but it was a bit of a hazardous business. Apart from the sea-sickness and being stuck for months on a big boat with a bunch of trainspotters, there was always the possibility that the boat might bump into something or spring a leak. The *Titanic* did both. However the sinking of the *Titanic* did have a good side, though not for the hundreds of people who died; the sinking led to lots of changes in boat safety, such as providing enough lifeboats, establishing better radio contact and trying to avoid icebergs. Meanwhile, the skies were filling up, and in...
1952 The first commercial airline service using a jet engine was started. Travel really started to take off!
1969 The first Jumbo Jet flew.

From then on cars got faster, aeroplanes got bigger, trains got dirtier and ships got their bottoms wet. Just imagine it – after a pretty slow start with nothing but a horse on wheels to get you around, suddenly there were any amount of different means of transport to choose from – even space rockets!

And it's pretty much the same story with...

The three Rs

Education has always been important. Even the ancient Romans realized that you had to go to school[1], although if you got too clever they fed you to the lions. But what about reading, writing and arithmetic, the basis of all learning? Well in...

c. 3500 BC Not content with inventing the wheel, the Sumerians turned their hand, to inventing the first written language. After all, what was the point of being able to invent clever things like wheels if you couldn't write and tell your mum about them? OK, so this language was little more than a series of pictures with no word for cul-de-sac, but it was a start.
c. 3400 BC Not to be outdone, the Egyptians developed a special symbol for the number ten. Before that all numbers were written down as single strokes, so for instance the number 47 would be 47 single strokes, 156 would be 156 single strokes, 1,789,876 would be ... well, I think you've got the idea! By having a symbol for ten you reduce the amount of writing considerably.

Thus 47 would now be four "ten" symbols followed by seven single strokes. It still took up a lot of room, but that didn't discourage them, and in...

1. Their school system was as comprehensive as the one we have now, with many of the really important things like bullying and truancy.

c. 2800 BC The Egyptians now cracked the problem of what to write all those numbers on to. They used papyrus, which came from a plant found on the banks of the Nile.
c. 1600 BC By this time the ancient Greeks had developed a language. Many of the words in our language have come from the Greek; like Doner Kebab, for instance.
1000 BC The Phoenicians invented a *phonetic* alphabet, which is the basis of our alphabet today.
500 BC The Chinese invented the abacus. They couldn't have known it, but this was the forerunner of the computer!

In ancient times education was far more popular in the East than it was in the West, and this continued into the next millennium. Take the Vikings, for instance. They weren't bothered that you couldn't write your name as long as you could take somebody's ear off with a throwing axe at 20 paces. So how did things change in...

The first millennium of school?

With Christianity becoming the main religion of the Roman Empire the need for education became more important, if only so that people could learn about God – or get killed in the attempt. As with many things, the

Chinese were still leading the field, although ironically they were having nothing to do with Christianity! Here's a couple of their major breakthroughs:

AD 105 Real paper - none of your papyrus nonsense! They probably used the bark of the mulberry tree, beat it to a pulp and then rolled it into sheets.

Unfortunately this form of paper didn't really catch on in Europe until the end of the millennium. Until then the rest of the world were still writing on papyrus, parchment or the back of their hands.

868 "OK, so maybe nobody wants our paper," thought the Chinese, but it didn't stop them inventing the first printing press and - not surprisingly - printing the first book. After all, what else would you do with a printing press?

Real paper! Proper printing! Whatever next? Well, let's look at...

The second millennium – a time of learning

Education continued to develop. Soon even *girls* would be allowed some! And then a new invention started its steady development. An invention that would change the face of the world for ever!

1617 A Scotsman, John Napier, invented *Napier's Bones*, to calculate logarithms. Although they looked more like lunch than a logs machine, they took us one (tiny) step nearer to computer science. Napier could not have had any idea of the impact computers would have on education. Likewise in...

1673 Gottlieb Von Leibniz wouldn't have realized the full potential when he invented a multiplying machine. It was a huge thing that worked on cogs turned by a handle, and it was still being used in the 1940s!

Then in...

1822 Charles Babbage brought computing one step nearer by inventing his Difference Machine. Babbage is considered the father of modern computers, although such things were unheard of in schools, even for writing. Most writing in schools was done with a quill pen, but that was changing.

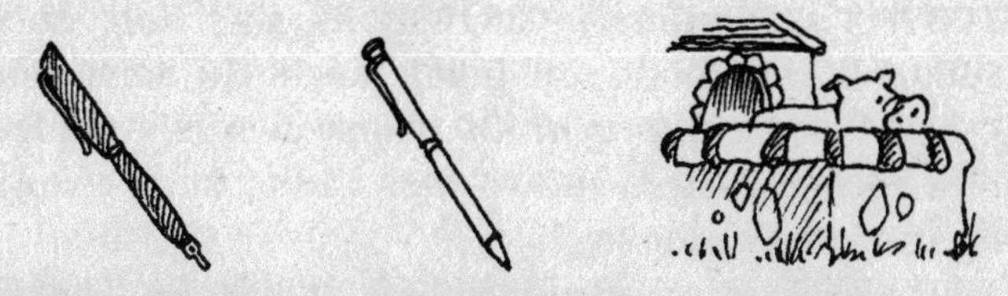

The biro was invented in 1943 by an Hungarian called Lazlo Biro - hence the name! I suppose it could have been worse - he could have been called Ramsbottom.

By...

1951 The first commercially available computers had been developed. They were mostly in libraries, businesses and some schools. Great! Real technology at last! The only problem was that most of them were the size of Cornwall! It was another 25 years before they would be small enough to fit on a desk.

Education continued to develop. Exams were introduced. It reached a point when you could hardly move in schools without getting tested. But at least a test was a test; you knew when it was going to happen and you could go sick. All that changed in...

1988 When GCSEs were introduced. Suddenly you were not just judged on your exam results, but on your school work as well; which meant that you had to start doing some!

1989 The National Curriculum was introduced. Suddenly everybody was being taught the same things – and being *compared*! Of course it was completely unworkable at first, and so they had to keep changing it. And keep changing it.

1991 SATs were introduced. It stands for Statutory Attainment Targets. Which meant that now they had a target by which you could be judged on the National Curriculum, which by now was totally confusing.

With no let-up in testing and exams, computers were introduced, and started to replace normal teaching aids in some schools. This was seen as The Way Forward. With the development of the Internet and World Wide Web, there was greater access to information than there had ever been before. Anything you needed to know – and plenty of things that you didn't – could be found with the click of a mouse. It became known as the Information Superhighway. It seemed that the potential for this information technology was endless, and again huge developments have been made. Things that the Chinese, when they were developing their printing press, could not even have dreamed of. And it's exactly the same story with…

Communication

Writing had a huge impact on communication between ancient civilizations. Or at least it would have done if reading had caught on in the same way. The main problem was that most people had their own language and didn't see the point of learning anyone else's, since you were probably more likely to want to fight them than to talk to them. After all, they were *foreigners.* But if anyone wanted to send a message to somebody else, the time-honoured method was to send a messenger. The most famous incidence of this was in…

490 BC When the Athenians had just defeated the Persians at Marathon. A Greek runner was sent to Athens to tell everyone the wonderful news. Unfortunately nobody bothered to tell him that it was about 26 miles, otherwise he might have said, "Well yes, of course, I *would* go, but I've got this dodgy knee you see, and…" But because they didn't tell him, he went.

Probably the worst job anyone could have was that of messenger, which was still the popular way of passing information, even in the first millennium. Popular, that is, with everyone except the messengers themselves. This was mainly due to the fact that if the message was bad you got killed on the spot, and if the message involved anyone doing anything about the message, you often got taken hostage until whatever had to be done about the message had been done.

Following so far? Good! Messengers were often high-born people, princes and so forth. The idea behind this was that the messenger had to be *worth* holding hostage. There's not a lot of point in going to the trouble of holding a messenger hostage if he's a nobody is there? That would be a bit like kidnapping the postman![1]

Communication around this time was still a word-of-mouth business. The Information Superhighway was a long way off. But in the second millennium things hotted up, and a lot of the stuff invented then will have a huge impact on the future. So let's see what's on offer:

1. Not that I'm suggesting that the postman is a nobody. Of course, I'm not. He's very important, especially if he's got a letter for me!

From then on more and more satellites were launched. Satellite television came into being, beaming dozens of channels around the world. Computers became more and more a part of the communications network, with fax, e-mail, and of course the good old WWW.

We now had the technology to communicate with almost anybody, almost anywhere in the universe, didn't we?

Ah yes! But what about...

Fashion?

Fashion hasn't always just been a series of silly hats and even sillier shoes, but in ancient times it was not the huge business that it is today. Then, people wore whatever they could get their hands on – animal skins mostly.

It was not really until the world developed that the need for fashion increased. And increase it certainly did. This was largely due to a number of key inventions.

Study this picture of a couple of average fashion victims, and then list all the labelled inventions in the order in which they were invented. Answers at the back of the book:

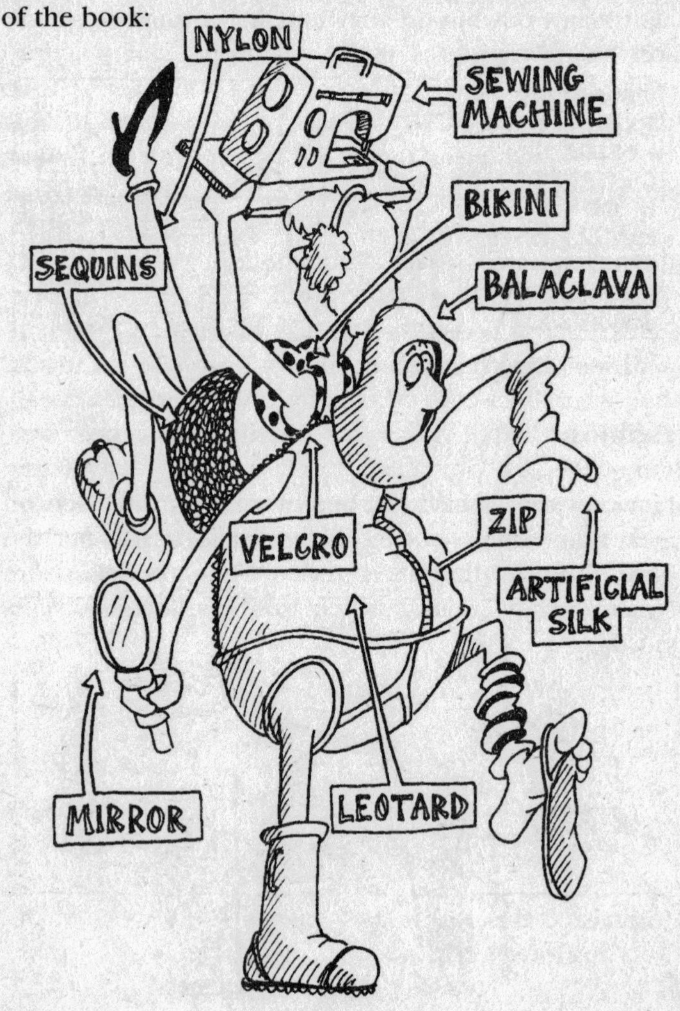

And all this before we all became obsessed with designer labels! Agh! Pass the sick bag! Or call the doctor! Funny I should say that, because we're about to dip into the doctor's bag, and take a look at…

Ancient medicine

This was administered pretty much on a "kill or cure" basis. If you were ill you were given a potion that either killed you or cured you. It was largely assumed that if the gods - whoever they were at the time - fancied curing you then you would get better, and if they didn't - well, tough! Medicine and hospitals as we know them today didn't really exist, although in…

c. 460 – 377 BC Hippocrates lived. Who was he then? A Greek doctor. Generally thought of as the "Father of Medicine". Which is why the doctor's promise not to talk about your diseases to other people - even to get a cheap laugh - is called the Hippocratic Oath[1]. Hippocrates was one of the first physicians to realize that diseases and injuries weren't always caused by evil spirits or Acts of God; they could be caused by the wrong diet, bad weather or getting run over by a passing chariot.

He realized this, but didn't always know what to do about it. However, in…

1. You probably thought that this was some sort of medical swearing. Well, it isn't!

c. 350 BC The Greeks established *aesculapia* - temples of Aesculapius, a healer who had lived about a thousand years earlier. People could come to these *aesculapia* in the hope of getting cured. The Romans established similar places; in fact the word "hospital" comes from the Latin *hospes*, which means host or guest. Hospitals were more like hotels full of sick people.

In both instances the invalid stayed there until they either got better or died. Or their money ran out. Sometimes they could be in there for years, unlike today. Today we have the technology to get people into hospital and kill them off in just a few hours. But what about…

The first millennium – trust me, I'm a doctor, probably!

Although advances had been made, medicine was still deeply rooted in religion and superstition. For example, when the Black Death swept through Europe in the 14th century, people were told that they wouldn't catch it if they believed in God. The numbers of people attending church shot up dramatically. Unfortunately so did the numbers of dead people.

One of the major differences between this period and the last was that, with the increase in travel and trading, the range of diseases that you could catch increased alarmingly. But just wait till we get to the...

Second millennium

Which we've just done! It only took a few inventions for medicine to start to make that Great Leap Forward. For instance, in...

1628 The circulation of the blood was discovered. And wow! Wasn't this a huge discovery! Before then doctors probably thought that your blood just sat around sulking in a corner of your body, waiting to escape through the first available hole if you accidentally cut yourself. This could explain why doctors still sometimes inject you in your bottom. Under the old theory, if you'd been sitting down for any length of time your blood would have collected in your bum. So naturally if a doctor wanted to get drugs into your bloodstream quickly, your bottom would be the obvious point of entry. It's a theory anyway. Personally I think that doctors only inject you in the bot to cause you as much humiliation as possible, but then, what do I know?

And, of course, once doctors discovered how blood worked there was no stopping them. A whole range of things that we take for granted today were introduced: inoculations, aspirins, insulin, penicillin, DNA, vaccines, heart transplants, artificial hearts, organ transplants, etc.

Doctors discovered that not only could they save life, but they could also create it. In 1978 the first "test-tube" baby was born. Less than 20 years later they had cloned a sheep. Where would it all end? We'd see later. But with all this new medical technology, people felt able to relax and enjoy themselves more. But how?

Leisure and sport

I expect you've often asked yourself what people did for fun before the telly was invented. No? Well, I'm going to tell you anyway. Conquering other countries and putting the locals to death in a variety of different ways was very popular. Then there was hunting for sport and food. Now we just do it for sport, but then *we've* got supermarkets.

The Greeks, being more sophisticated than most, held their Olympic Games. Or at least they did when they weren't too busy attacking other people. Of course, there were a whole range of sports and activities that passed the time and helped you forget that you'd had no lunch; well, nothing edible anyway. Here are a few taken from early art:

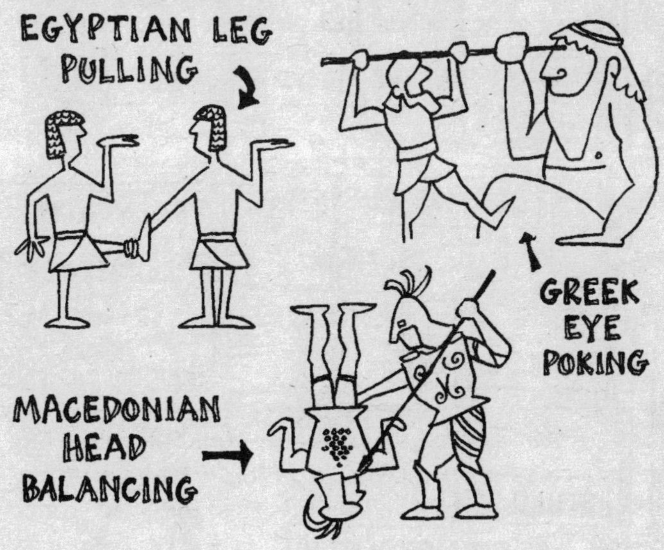

Oh yes, as your grandparents are probably fond of saying, "We had to make our own amusement in those days!"

Well, as we'll see, the age of technology has changed all this quite considerably. But not as much as we might like to think, certainly not in the first millennium. It wasn't until the second millennium that the things that will ultimately affect our future first saw the light of day. But when were they invented? Take a look at the picture overleaf and see if you can put the items that are labelled in the order in which they first came into being. The answers are in the back of the book.

Of course in more recent years things have just snowballed: CDs, games machines (such as Playstation and Gameboy), in-line skates, skateboards, mountain bikes – oh, the list is endless. But where will we be in the next century? We'll have to wait to find out, because first we have to look at...

Exploration

Exploring in ancient times had a great deal to do with finding a better place to live. For instance, as long ago as…

30,000 BC Mongoloid hunters from Asia crossed a great ice age land bridge to settle in America. And they'd never even *heard* of Christopher Columbus!

The other important reason for exploring was to find new people to conquer and lands to steal; or other nations to trade with. The spice trade was flourishing. Although the need to trade (and conquer people) still exists today, there's much more of a sense of exploration for its own sake. Space travel, for example, has more to do with seeing what's up there than it does with anything else, although the theory is that one day it will come in handy. We'll see from the predictions for the 21st century (later in the book) just how true this is!

Throughout the first millennium, exploration was still pretty well a case of getting in a boat and saying, "I wonder what's over there?" Of course, many people thought that the world was flat, and if an expedition of discovery was sent out and never returned (because they were killed, eaten by wolves or abducted by aliens) the people left behind assumed that they'd fallen off the edge of the world.

"See?" they'd say. "That's what comes of having fancy travelling ideas! We're much better off staying where we are!"

Luckily for us, not everybody had this attitude. The Romans, for instance, were only too happy to explore the world, take it over and give everyone proper plumbing. Other great civilizations had tried this and largely failed. Some of them were rapidly disappearing anyway. It wasn't until the next millennium that major exploration discoveries started to be made. I suppose a major one would be...

1492 Christopher Columbus "discovered" America. Of course it had been there all the time, it's just that he didn't know that. It's also quite likely that the Vikings had already been there, but they hadn't made such a big fuss about it.

Once the known world had pretty well been explored, man (and woman) turned their attention to the skies, in much the same way as they had done with transport. In...

1781 The planet Uranus was discovered. Of course, all they could do is look at it through a telescope. They couldn't go there. It wasn't until...

1957 That the first ever spacecraft was launched, by the Russians. It was called *Sputnik1*. Not to be outdone, the Americans followed in 1958 with *Explorer 1*, and so the race to be first on the Moon began. Over the next two decades more than 1,600 spacecraft were launched, and in...

1969 The first men (Americans) landed on the Moon. They claimed it was "one small step for man, one giant leap for mankind". They didn't say whether or not it was made of cheese.

Since then the Space Race has been scaled down a bit due to money, but it still goes on. Other countries have joined in (including Britain), presumably because they want to be the first to land somewhere – Mars, Jupiter, anywhere! Some countries are even planning to fly to the Sun, and in order to avoid being burnt to a crisp, they're planning to go at night[1]. Whether this space travel will have any practical use remains to be seen.

Likewise, whether or not there's life on other planets will also be discovered, possibly. Frankly, I think that a quick look round your average supermarket would tell you that there is no life on other planets – they've already come down to Earth!

1. You realize that this is not true, don't you? Oh, please tell me you do!

But how will any of this affect our…

Lifestyle?

This is the term currently used in *Medialand* to cover anything to do with the way we live, from fridges and frozen peas to raves and rambling. In ancient times lifestyle was pretty well dictated by where you lived, how cold it was and how many foreigners were trying to kill you. But here's a couple of dates to give us a starting point:

c. 2737 BC The Chinese discovered tea. That is to say that some Chinaman discovered that if you crush the leaves of the tea plant and mix it with boiling water, it makes a nice drink. The question is what was he *trying* to discover?
2600 BC The Egyptians discovered how to make leavened bread. Before that they had to make do with a medium sliced loaf from the milkman.
c. 1400 BC The Egyptians invented water-operated clocks. It was a complex thing as you can see…

Of course, the first millennium was largely dominated by the spread of Christianity and other organized religions. Suddenly people discovered that much of their lifestyle was "wrong". Not that it stopped them, and when the second millennium came along, they discovered numerous things that previously they could only dream about.

By travelling around to other countries and meeting with other cultures, they discovered other foods. OK, so these foods lost some of their original charm in travelling – an eastern dish marinated for weeks in a hundred different spices became a boil-in-the-bag curry – but cultures were sharing their knowledge. As technology increased so did the range of products that now affect our lifestyle. Some of these are already included in the little quiz in the **Leisure and sport** section, so we don't need to go into too much detail here. All we really need to say is that, given the rate at which our own lifestyles have changed in the last few years, we can expect major changes during the next century.

War, religion and politics

No book about the future would be complete without a section detailing the major world events that have helped shape our past, present and future.

Except this one.

Even those of you with the scantiest knowledge of history will know about the key world events[1], such as the First and Second World Wars, known as the Great War, and ... er ... the 39/45 War. Of course, you must realize that history books will eventually rename these wars *The Greatest War in the World EVER* and *The Greatest War in the World EVER II*[2].

It's also a fact that there is at least one war taking place all the time, although not the same one obviously.

1. Unless, like me, you were looking out of the window when history was being taught.
2. Or *Now That's What I Call Killing I & II.*

In fact, I think that statistics suggest that there are 26 wars happening worldwide at any given time. Now these could be anything from two super powers in the grip of a nuclear stand-off, or two blokes in anoraks fighting over a parking space.

Either way, they need not concern us now. All we need to bear in mind is that politics and religion will have an important role to play in the future of our planet. That said, we can move on.

Let's do the time warp again

When you study the potted history above, you see a pattern emerging. See it? No? Let me explain then. In ancient times things move forward fairly steadily, and it isn't really until the second half of the second millennium that things start to really speed up; in many cases developing so fast that it's hard to keep track of them.

Not in all cases, obviously. For instance – why did it take so long to invent the tea bag? After all, the Chinese invented tea in 2,737 BC, and paper in AD 105; two major breakthroughs by an obviously sophisticated culture. So why did it take until 1920 for somebody to wrap some tea in paper and invent the tea bag?

On the other hand, let's look at computers: a hundred years ago the only thing that they had that even remotely resembled a computer was a huge complicated adding machine. Even the computers of 60 years ago were so big that they took up entire buildings. Now we have computers that sit on a desk (or even in your hand!) and can be operated by just touching the screen. And all in the space of comparatively few years.

This is a perfect example of the way technology works; once somebody makes that initial breakthrough things take off. And we need to bear this in mind when we're thinking about the future. We also need to realize that some technology has gone about as far as it can go for the time being, and so not everything will continue to develop at the sort of pace that it's developing at now. But what exactly does the future hold? Time to call in the experts!

My team is hand-picked ... like my nose

When picking a team of experts to help unravel the mysteries of the future, a number of questions spring to mind. After all, this is unlike any assignment I have ever undertaken. Here I am about to go into the totally unknown with not so much as a packed lunch.

Oh yes, of course, I will be able to make some pretty informed guesses based on the previous history section, but if I'm to provide you, my loyal reader, with everything you need in order to cope with the century ahead of you, I am going to have to do better than a few clever guesses, or even a lot of stupid ones. I am going to need genuine expert opinion, from genuine experts. But how will I find them?

Approaching the whole thing scientifically I drew up a list of the sort of qualities my "experts" would need. I did this carefully, methodically, and dispassionately. No favouritism - my team had to be the best.

In just a matter of months I had the definitive list of qualities that a team of this importance would have to have. The reason it took so long is because I realized that this was an important project, not something that I could take lightly. It needed a serious and professional attitude. And it was with all this in mind that I carefully drew up my list. Then I lost the old envelope that I'd written the list on and had to start again. But I finally had a definitive document. Just to give you some idea of the complexity of the task, I'm going to print my final list here and now, so that you can see just exactly what I had to go through in the process of picking my team of experts:

Qualities required for expert in researching the future...
1, will they be able to turn up on thursday?
2, Will they pay their own bus fare to my house?
3, will they bring their own coffee/tea etc?
4. Will they want paying?
5, Will I be able to get anyone else if they can't do it?
MILK
SUGAR
DOG FOOD

Sorry – I don't know what the last three items refer to.

Confident that I had covered every angle, I set about selecting my team. After much soul-searching, bribery and arguments with the milkman, the final team was whittled down to:

Elderado Dingbatti

Although a loyal supporter of my work for many years[1], I had no idea that I would be able to get him on my team. I didn't even realize that he'd been released. But then I suppose that's what care in the community is all about. Certainly Elderado's social worker was extremely pleased that I

1. He often says to me, "What do you do for a living, then?"

was able to offer him a permanent address and some worthwhile employment.

Elderado was extremely disappointed that I wasn't able to offer him a fully-qualified nursing staff and a hospital in the Crimea, but that was only because he currently believed himself to be Florence Nightingale, the "lady with the lamp". After a few weeks of sleeping on my sofa he would be the "lady with the cramp", though what my neighbours would say about him walking around in his nurse's uniform I don't know.

They weren't too happy when I built a pond for my koi carp in the back garden, although that might have been due to the fact that we discovered that the carp weren't coy at all. In fact they weren't carp – they were piranhas, which frankly I think is a very unusual thing for an Avon Lady to be selling door-to-door.

Actually, I'm very grateful to my neighbours for discovering that my new fish were so dangerous. Well, it wasn't them that discovered it; it was their pet Cairn terrier, Thompson, but only because he fell into the pond. They keep asking for his collar back, but you won't catch me dipping my hand in that pond – not for long anyway!

Be that as it may, there was something very comforting about having a member of the nursing profession on my team, even if it was only my mad friend dressed up.

His role on the team was that of communications expert and spiritual support. He answered the phone and made the coffee.

Patrick (Paddy) O'Dors

Paddy O'Dors, a discharged conservatory salesman, has been staring at the stars for years, or at least he was until he was caught staring at the woman who plays Betty in *Emmerdale* in a supermarket. He assured me that he had a keen interest in heavenly bodies, which naturally I took to mean the planets. However, he is a resourceful man, and it took him hardly any time at all (seven years) to grasp the basics of planetary fortune-telling.

In fact, before I could say, "What the heck do you think you're doing?" he had half my roof off and had converted the loft into a miniature planetarium. My mum wasn't too pleased. But Paddy, like many Irish people, has that wonderful Celtic charm that can melt the hardest heart. That, plus the fact that he cried every time she told him off, meant that he got away with it.

Mum obviously wasn't too happy when he started charging the neighbours to come round and look at the Milky Way through his telescope, but that was probably due to the fact that he'd told them that a slap-up feed was included in the price.

I still shudder to think of my poor mum baking six dozen individual steak pies, whilst half the street stared in awe through the telescope at the galaxy. How none of them ever spotted the fact that the galaxy was actually a chocolate wrapper on the end of a stick amazes me. But then when all is said and done we were providing a service, and the money came in handy for "research purposes"[1].

Mrs Wibley

You may wonder how this woman ever found her way back on to a research team of mine after the way we fell out last time. You may also wonder how she found her way back from Scotland after the way she fell out of the back of her new husband's reconditioned furniture van. He'd taken her away on honeymoon, which took the form of a driving tour of the Highlands. But, what with having the van and Mrs Wibley being so keen on ironing, it seemed silly not to kill two birds with one stone by setting up a mobile laundry service. The fact that they actually killed two hedgehogs with one very large falling woman could not have been foreseen. But then if the interior light hadn't failed, poor Mrs Wibley wouldn't have been ironing in the back of the van with the doors open as her husband, who thinks he's Damon Hill, took a sharp corner at 75 miles an hour.

It could have been far more serious; those winding Highland roads have sheer drops on either side. Fortunately, they were passing a loch and Mrs W is a

1. Trips to the chippy when we got sick of steak pie.

good swimmer. Mercifully the paintwork on the van wasn't damaged at all, so sighs of relief all round.

Of course, I could have refused to have her on the team. At least I could have done if I was prepared to spend the rest of my life living under an assumed name and a large tarpaulin. So I welcomed her back with open arms. I convinced myself that she would be really useful. I was wrong.

Neville the Psychic Cockle

I must admit that on our first meeting Neville looked more like a winkle than a cockle, but I was assured that that was because he is small for his age, plus the fact that psychic prediction can really take its toll, particularly if all you're normally used to doing is lying around in the sea and sticking to boats.

Neville was at the height of his fame in 1998, when the film *Titanic* was released. He apparently had a relative called Sebastian who had gone down on the *Titanic*, and this made Neville a must for any chat show that year. Sebastian's story was almost more tragic and romantic than the *Titanic* disaster itself; apparently he'd fallen in love with a rivet he'd mistaken for a female cockle, and despite many pleas from other marine life, he refused to leave "her". Sadly he perished in those cold grim depths, when a passing whale accidentally ate him.

On the *Michael Parkinson Show* Kate Winslet, the star of *Titanic*, was so moved by Neville's story that she proposed to him on the spot. He turned her down, because he was in love with Phillipa Forrester, having got stuck to her bottom in a lift during a recording of *Tomorrow's World*.

It was on the *Parkinson Show* that Neville's extraordinary psychic powers were revealed. Parkinson had a nasty head cold, and literally seconds before he did it, Neville called out (through his interpreter Dave Dilks), "Watch out! He's gonna sneeze!"

Everyone agreed – or at least said "maybe" – that this revealed true psychic powers, and had nothing whatever to do with the fact that "Parky" had just thrown back his head, gone "Ah-ah-ah...", pulled out his hanky and said, "Excuse me." Thus – like so many famous people – Neville's reputation was made overnight. Although of course he wasn't a person, he was a cockle. But that made it all the more remarkable.

Unfortunately what made it all the more complicated was the simple fact that Neville's psychic urges could only really be induced when he (and everybody else in the room) was immersed in a tank of sea water. This made playing cards very difficult, which was a pity because almost half of our research time was taken up doing precisely that. I quickly learned deep sea diver's hand signals for "I've got a pair" and "What beats a royal flush?", which I'm sure will come in handy one day.

In order to make Neville's "undoubted" skills more

accessible, we devised a "psychic environment" for him. This consisted of a children's paddling pool full of brine, plus a set of "plastic finish" tarot cards. It wasn't ideal, but at least it stopped my shoes rotting.

It was during a particularly tricky psychic session that I noticed a very strange thing about Neville: he moved very, very slowly – if at all. I'd almost say that he was totally stationary; at least he was when anyone was watching. But if you turned away, and then turned back, Neville could quite easily be on the other side of the pool sitting on the Grim Reaper, whereas he'd previously been on the Four of Cups[1]. I mentioned this to Dave, who was wiping his hands on the tablecloth – an action that I took to be a nervous habit since he did it so often, especially just after Neville had made a major underwater movement. With a large sigh, which I took as an insult, Dave said: "It is not for us mere mortals to question the mysterious ways of the psychic." Mrs Wibley nodded in agreement, as did Paddy O'Dors. Elderado said: "Drop your trousers – it's time for your cough medicine."

I know when I'm outnumbered.

1. Tarot cards, naturally!

Nostradamus

Now, I bet you're saying: "Oh come on! How did you manage to get a 16th-century mystic on to your research team?", unless you're on the bus, in which case you're probably just thinking it. Let me explain. We didn't actually have him in the room with us. After all, he's been dead for several centuries, and so his presence in the room would have done nothing for the level of air pollution, although it might have helped to disguise the overpowering smell of furniture polish[1]. Also the presence of anything dead in the room causes the dog to run in circles chasing his tail and singing in a way that Michael Jackson would spend billions of dollars on major larynx surgery to achieve.

The fact is that we contacted Nostradamus from beyond the grave. By which I don't mean that we sent him a letter addressed to "Nostradamus (Mr), Beyond The Grave, Heaven/Hell, HE2 1GD". Of course we didn't! What do you take us for – morons?

Actually we did, but when he hadn't replied after two months we decided to try another method. Let me explain further:

Having convinced ourselves that he was the only person who could reveal the true secrets of the future to us, but having read his book and not understood a

1. Mum loves housework.

word of it, we were completely stumped[1].

It was at this point that Mrs Wibley said: "I'm a medium, you know." We all looked at her. She was an extra large if she was anything, and even then we're talking Marks and Spencer's which are always cut on the big side. I was about to point this out when she explained, saving me a lot of embarrassment, not to mention a whack over the head from one of the army surplus woks she was juggling at the time. "I can get in touch with people from the other side," she said.

"What? Basingstoke?" said Dave Dilks, whose grasp of the paranormal wasn't what it should be for someone who makes an extremely good living interpreting the psychic actions of an undernourished cockle.

"I've got a friend in the Royal Free Hospital in Frimley," commented Elderado, as he practised a Werther's splint on the leg of the coffee table.

"No! I mean I can contact dead people!" exclaimed an exasperated Mrs W.

"I knew that," I lied.

And thus it was that we found ourselves holding hands and humming. The police were very nice about it, although I suppose it must have looked strange. After all, it's not every day that even the police see six people and a cockle sitting in a circle, holding hands and humming. Especially when one of them looked every inch like a man in drag, even if that was Mrs Wibley[2].

1. That is to say, I was completely stumped. We were having a quick game of indoor cricket and I was batting, until Neville the cockle caused me to be run out on account of his extremely slow movement.
2. Elderado looked surprisingly convincing as a woman, but then those early nurses' uniforms were never very flattering.

I think the only mistake that the young "copper" made was mentioning this fact to her. Once we'd lifted him into his squad car and assured him that the ringing in his ears would die off quite soon – after all it was only a wok, and how hard could a woman like Mrs Wibley realistically hit? – he seemed quite forgiving. But ever since, just to be on the safe side, I always make sure I do every hand signal in the Highway Code (and some that aren't) when I'm out on my bike; policemen have long memories. And silly helmets.

Anyway, after several attempts we finally got through to the "other side". The first person we spoke to was the famous American Indian, Geronimo, who went on and on about the number of dead parachutists who came up to him and blamed him for the fact that they had hit the ground before their parachute had opened. He couldn't even understand why they should want to shout his name as they jumped out of planes, although he was quite flattered. "Is it my fault that I've got a long name?" He whinged on for about ten minutes until General Custer came up and demanded a rematch.

Then we got Napoleon who complained about the number of lunatics who go around pretending to be him. It turned out that he wasn't even the real Napoleon, just another lunatic impersonating him, which was a bit of a disappointment.

We briefly contacted Florence Nightingale which threw poor Elderado into a bit of a state, and in fact we were about to give the whole thing up as a waste of time when – clear as a bell – we heard:

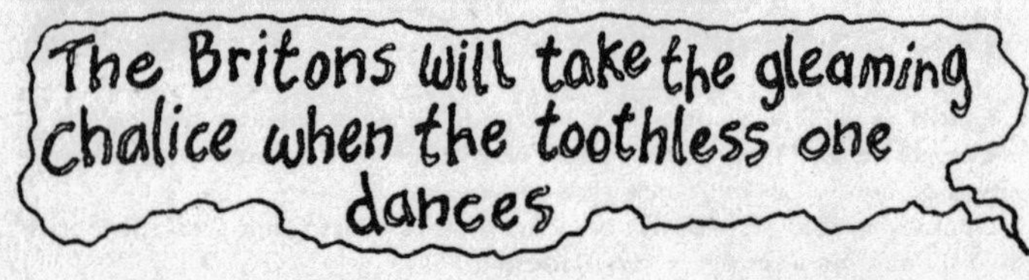

At first this meant nothing, but then Dave, who just happened to have the lyrics of *Three Lions* tattooed on his left instep, said: "Of course! It's the 1966 World Cup!" And then it all became clear; the toothless one referred to Nobby Stiles, who took his teeth out to play in the match, and – according to the song – danced ("and Nobby dancing"). The gleaming chalice was obviously the Jules Rimet Trophy ("Jules Rimet still gleaming") which the Britons took by winning the match.

Brilliant! Nostradamus had the gift! Weren't we lucky to have him on our team! Frankly, we were ecstatic. Even the fact that we were completely wrong about his message didn't dull our enthusiasm. Wrong? Yes, wrong! It turned out that he wasn't talking about the 1966 World Cup at all. He'd never even *heard* about it. He was actually referring to his toothless old granny's 80th birthday party, and the fact that the entire event was ruined when – during the disco – some English tourists broke in and pinched the family silver, and after she'd just polished it as well ("gleaming chalice")!

He then went on about what a pain Heaven was because people kept coming up and asking him to predict things, like what they would be having for tea; which was stupid because as everybody knows tea in Heaven is always manna, with a chocolate digestive if you're really lucky.

"And as if *that* isn't bad enough, there's this Napoleon bloke who..." We let Nostradamus ramble on for a bit. After all, it was either that or watching *Telly Addicts.*

Whether ultimately he was a useful member of the team will be revealed as I show how we used our collective powers to unravel the mysteries of the years ahead.

A rune with a view

Once the team had been put together we started work. Soon my bedroom had been turned into our headquarters. The walls were covered with blown-up versions of my timelines and historic fact-files, of which I was justifiably proud. Since there was no available wall space, the ceiling was covered in the astrological charts being drawn up by Paddy O'Dors. Neville's "psychic environment" was set up on my computer table, and finally there was a small card table at which Mrs Wibley would be spending many a long hour casting runes.

Sorry, did I say runes? I actually meant scrabble tiles. When I questioned this Mrs W said (rather testily, I thought), "Have you seen the price of runes these days?" I had to admit that I hadn't. "And anyway, these will work just as well."

I wasn't convinced about the truth of this last statement. And I think that my fears were proved founded because, when the runes were cast to answer the question "Will the hole in the ozone layer eventually cause the end of the world?", the answer seemed to be "xylophone".

This excited everyone greatly, for some reason.

Everyone except me, that is. When I asked them what all the fuss was about, they pointed out, as though talking to a cabbage, that if only "xylophone" had been cast on a scrabble board instead of a card table, it would have made 201 points with a triple word score. It was obvious that working with this particular team was going to be an uphill struggle.

We get down to business

Despite all our set-backs we finally got down to business. A daily routine was soon established. Once Elderado had checked our pulses and asked if we'd opened our bowels, we opened the post and then got going on the business of the day. Choosing the same areas to examine that I had in my potted history (which was a blessing!) we used all methods at our disposal to try and predict the future.

What follows are the fruits of our labours. Where possible I've tried to indicate how we arrived at our findings, and offered suggestions as to how you can cope with everything that the future – or at least the next century – is going to throw at you. And when I say throw, I do mean throw! So let's get on with…

Coping with the 21st Century

As you'll see, I've broken the century into handy ten-year bites, and then listed the various categories covered in the earlier section. Each entry will have its own icon, and then be divided into three subheadings, as shown below:

EFFECT
This tells you what effect, if any, the prediction is likely to have on you.

COPING
This offers advice about how to cope with the effects of the prediction.

PREDICTION SOURCE
This lets you know how my team arrived at their prediction. Sometimes this will simply say *historic* which means that the prediction has been arrived at by studying the past and making an educated guess. (Well, a guess anyway!)

Clear? Right! Let's go for it!

NOTE: It will not have escaped your attention, particularly if you have a basic understanding of the concept of *time*, that – as the next century progresses – you will get older. My team has tried to bear this in mind while making our predictions, so that everything is as relevant to you as possible. We've also tried to include things that will affect people who are the same age as you are now, but in the future. Can you follow that? Good! Can you explain it to me, please? Anyway, the thing for you to do is to select the entries that apply to you and ignore the rest. For the purposes of this next section I'll be referring to you as *you*, whether you regard yourself as an adult, a child or something in between. Thank you so much. Now read on!

2000 – 2010

This will be an important time for you. During these ten years you'll be making big decisions about your future. You'll be moving through school, college or university, and maybe even out the other end into the Big World. You might be leaving home, but if you're lucky you'll be able to bring your laundry back at weekends. Of course, if you're really crafty you might even be able to bring several of your friends' laundry back with you too!

After all, you'll need to supplement those student grants[1] somehow! And talking of surviving on a restricted budget, let's consider what sort of future this ten-year period holds for…

MONEY

Just as 2000 BC spelt the end of cattle as currency and the beginning of coins, so AD 2000 will mark the end of coins, as – towards the end of the decade – the whole world is caught in the grip of "mad coins" disease. You've probably already noticed that coins are getting smaller and smaller. Well, by 2010 they'll be so small that they'll be completely invisible to the naked eye. This will be a great boon for parents, who will use this fact to avoid paying you pocket money. The conversation will go something like this…

1. Soon to be renamed the *People's Learning Credit*.

And, of course, a quick look at her will prove that she's telling the truth – she is indeed not made of money. But I bet you a pound (or at least I would if I could *see* one) that she's telling a big porky about putting the pocket money on the table.

So what will replace money? In a word – plastic. Yes! The credit, debit, store and loyalty card bonanza that started in the 1990s will continue, until there is a card for absolutely everything, including (eventually) going to school (see 2010–2020). Towards the end of the 2010s the average person could find themselves carrying anything up to 200 plastic cards.

EFFECT

Well, apart from everyone walking tilted to the left (or right depending on which pocket they carry their cards in), and apart from it taking seven times longer to get served in shops because of each customer having to sort through for the correct card, the impact on "young people" won't be that great. What will affect you more, however, is the loss of coins and the subsequent loss of pocket money. That will really hit your pocket. Well, not your pocket obviously, because that will be empty.

COPING

The answer is simple: electronic banking! This will be far more widespread by then, although adults will have no more idea about how it works than they do now. They'll have even less idea if anything. And this is where being a Child of the Computer Generation is really going to come in handy. Say to your dad (or mum): "Look, don't bother to give me any pocket money. It only causes a row when one of us accidentally drops it and it disappears under a grain of salt. Just set up an electronic bank account for me, and transfer my pocket money into it every week." They are almost certain to say, "Gosh! That sounds very complicated", to which you say, "Then leave it to me. Just pop your bank details on this scrap of paper, with a sample of your signature, and I'll do the rest!" You'll be amazed how well this works!

PREDICTION SOURCE

Historic. Just look at the last few years, and frankly you don't need a crystal ball to see that the above prediction is totally accurate. Not that that didn't stop my panel of "experts" getting out the crystal ball and doing a bit of gazing. Being a very sophisticated crystal ball they were about to pick up the TV shopping channel on it and buy a really handy foldaway multi-gym that fits into your back pocket; it makes you look great but it also makes it impossible to sit down.

TRAVEL

There's virtually nowhere else to go on this planet, but the first ten years of the next century won't see any big changes in space travel, either. Richard Branson will have generated enough personal hot air to be able to fly around the world *without* a balloon.

But apart from that we will be concentrating on reducing the amount of traffic on our roads rather than looking for new places to pollute. The first, and most obvious, step will be to pedestrianize more streets, particularly in the centre of towns and cities.

EFFECT

This is both a good and a bad thing for you. The bad thing is that you won't be able to get your parent to drop you off in town without having to walk part of the way. The *good* thing about this is that you can arrange to meet your parent at some convenient place, and they won't need to know where you've been!

COPING

Make sure that wherever you *actually* want to go, the place you tell your parents that you're going is right in the middle of a pedestrianized area.

PREDICTION SOURCE

Again this is historic. Past events indicate that something will have to be done about overcrowded roads very, very soon.

THE THREE Rs

Literacy hour, coupled with numeracy hour, introduced in 1998–9, will have been such a success that the Government – now renamed the People's Government (because it's made up of people) – will decide to extend this to other school subjects. First history hour, then geography hour, will be introduced. Biology, German, French, Latin and PE hours will follow.

You don't need to be a mathematical genius[1] to work out that these changes will lengthen the school day extensively. But don't worry. The Education Authorities (sorry, People's Learning Authorities) will quickly get on the case. They'll set up a committee to form a committee to advise a committee to appoint a committee to look into having a committee to sort it out. At the end of all this, which will take most of the decade, a solution will be found: lunch hour will be renamed lunch three minutes. Literacy and Numeracy hours will be abandoned as being too time-consuming.

1. Although thanks to numeracy hour, you probably will be.

EFFECT

When the bell goes at the end of the school day, you should just about have time to eat the lunch you couldn't manage to stuff down during lunch three minutes before the bell goes for the start of the next school day.

COPING

Since you won't really have time to go home, you could apply for a Student Credit Loan, now called the People-Who-Are-Students Credit Loan, in order to pay for a small foldaway bedsit that would fit into your school desk.

These will have been developed by the Japanese in order to help solve the growing homelessness problem. They'll come fully equipped with cooking and washing facilities[1]. You'll never have to put up with your parents trying to do your homework for you again!

PREDICTION SOURCE

Historic. Changes to the National Curriculum introduced throughout the 1990s indicate clearly that this is going to happen. Really!

1. Which will allow you to wash and cook at the same time, in the same bowl – a sort of wok with shower attachment.

COMMUNICATION ☎

This is the digital generation, and nowhere will this be felt more than in the world of communication. Mobile phones will continue to be bad for you, and so everyone – including very young children – will own several, colour-coordinated to your mood, the days of the week, whatever you want. They'll still be unnecessarily expensive but – what the heck – these are fashion items as much as anything!

The most sophisticated ones will be able to tell the caller that you're not there but that it'll tell you that they've called. *And then not bother*. This will be known as Tough Mode, because it'll be tough on callers. Just think of the money – sorry, plastic – you'll save on non-returned calls!

EFFECT

Losing friends will never be easier, so watch out.

COPING

Don't let the technology do the work for you. If you want to hang on to your mates (and who knows, you may need them one day!) then avoid Tough Mode.

PREDICTION SOURCE

Nostradamus. At least we think it was him. When we tried to contact him we got a strange, heavenly voice saying: "The person you are calling knows you are waiting. Please hold the line." We naturally took this to be some sort of cryptic message to do with the future of the telephone. After all, it's pretty unlikely Heaven has got *call waiting*. Or is it?

FASHION

Fashion will continue to be a minefield, with designers still calling the shots but making you think that you thought of it first. As for what the best-dressed person will be wearing, well it'll be rather a case of pick a day, any day, and check.

EFFECT

Much as it is now, only worse. You'll never keep up with changing fashion.

COPING

Don't bother. Follow your instinct and wear what you feel comfortable in. You'll still get pointed at whatever you do.

PREDICTION SOURCE

We picked Thursday 24 November 2009, and asked Neville the psychic cockle (who is a bit of a fashion guru in crustacean circles, according to Dave Dilks) to

do his stuff. Here's what he came up with:
In: Bobble hats, lemon-coloured duffel coats and anything made of seaweed.
Out: Flares.
He also warned us that it would all change by Friday the 25 November.

MEDICINE

The bad news is that waiting lists for even the simplest operation will now run to several years. The good news is that they will have discovered a cure for the common cold. The other bad news is that the common cold will no longer exist because it's been cured. It will have been replaced by the uncommon cold, which - unlike the now non-existent common one - will be incurable.

EFFECT

None of this will help you in the slightest. You'll still catch colds and doctors will still tell you that there's no cure.

COPING

There's a saying: "An apple a day keeps the doctor away." Keep a huge bowlful handy, and if you see a doctor coming towards you, throw them at him!

LEISURE / SPORT

The key to sporting success will continue to be sponsorship. Because of the huge increase in TV channels, and only so many old episodes of *Only Fools and Horses* to fill them up with, every sport will now be televised, and therefore attract sponsorship. And when I say "every", I do mean *every* – which is probably why I said it.

EFFECT

You won't be able to even have a game of tag without somebody wanting to film it.

COPING

Get yourself an agent who can really negotiate for you – i.e. not your Uncle Frank. Oh, and get a decent sponsor. The Ho Ming takeaway, Basildon, is not really international enough. Sorry.

PREDICTION SOURCE

Historic. As I write, TV companies and satellite companies are trying to get their hands on the Test Match. So by the year 2005 they'll be after anything that you can point a TV camera at.

EXPLORATION

The Space Race will continue being as pointless as it is costly. Almost as if the astronauts realize how pointless it is, the windscreens of spacecraft will carry stickers saying things like *I've seen the craters of Mercury*, and *Astronauts do it in zero gravity*. Do what, that's what I'd like to know; every film of astronauts in space that I've ever seen has them floating about bumping into each other. How they don't crash into something beats me. After all, if you were doing that sort of thing on the school bus there'd really be trouble.

Closer to the ground, our own planet will be combed for hidden supplies of natural resources; oil, coal, gas, Weetabix – that sort of thing.

Oil will be a major worry. Those countries that haven't got it will be desperately seeking it; those that have will be refusing to let anyone else have it – mainly because other people keep attacking them.

A large supply of natural gas will be discovered in an unusual place, sparking a panic similar to the Klondike Gold Rush of the 1860s.

EFFECT

Well, unless you live anywhere near Canal Street, Cheam, it won't affect you in the slightest. If you do then you could see your neighbourhood turned into a power station.

COPING

Move. Or stay where you are, depending on where you live in the first place.

PREDICTION SOURCE

Well, strange though it may seem, my team actually have pre-knowledge that this will happen, because the gas will in fact be discovered in Mrs Wibley's back garden. It's there now. I can tell you this because you won't be able to do anything about it without her phone number. This is how gas was discovered under her patio: during a quiet time, whilst Dave Dilks was trying to prise Neville off a tarot card[1] that he was making a particular mess of (I hate to say what he thought he was doing), Mrs Wibley – having caught the prediction bug – decided to try her hand at divining. She took a birch twig – well actually a couple of chopsticks sellotaped together – and went out into the garden to divine for natural spring water (sparkling preferably, with just a hint of apple).

It was a bitterly cold day, but she insisted on going

1. The card was *Fortitude*, which symbolizes power and energy, so I suppose it could have been a sign.

out in a short-sleeved blouse (and grass skirt, for some reason). Anyway, no sooner was she on the patio than the chopsticks started to twitch frantically.

Elderado diagnosed it as St Vitus's dance and offered to give her a vinegar rub, but Mrs W was convinced that this meant that there was a large supply of natural gas under her patio. She immediately sent for her husband who came home from work, bringing with him his pneumatic drill (what possible use a National Health dentist would have for a pneumatic drill I can't fathom, but still).

Anyway, in no time at all he had the patio up, but couldn't find the gas. By now it was getting dark, and Dave – who had elected himself Mrs W's agent and was therefore keen to see a result – suggested that we strike a match to help us see. But Mrs W wasn't having any of it, fortunately. She said that the gas would still be there in ten years' time. Twenty even. What she decided to do was wait until there was a world shortage of gas, which could happen at any minute, and then sell to the highest bidder. And that's what she's going to do, unless of course she dies first.

LIFESTYLE

As I mentioned earlier this will be the digital age, and nothing will be affected more than television. There will be hundreds of channels to choose from, all showing more or less the same programmes. The great thing about this is that, if you have to go to the loo during your favourite programme, you'll be able to switch channels and catch up where you left off five minutes later (or even ten minutes if you like taking your time in the toilet). The downside will be that if you want to just sit and watch the box, you may not be able to find a programme that you haven't already seen.

EFFECT
Deciding what to watch, and then being able to find it, will take up most of the day.

COPING
Employ/con/threaten a younger brother or sister to find your favourite programme for you, then call you when it starts. This is tricky and may cost lots.

PREDICTION SOURCE
Historical. In fact, it's already happening.

2011 - 2020

By now school and college will probably be a thing of the past for you, unless you're planning to become a teacher, in which case you'll *never* escape school. During this time you might even decide to settle down and get married. I never understand why people say that. I mean you can get married without settling down, and likewise you can settle down and not get married. I'm not even sure what people mean by "settling down" in the first place. Besides, this bit of the 20th century might be too exciting for anyone to want to even *think* about settling down, even if they can *afford* to. Which brings us neatly back to...

MONEY

The Pound In Your Pocket lobby will continue to campaign for a return to coins. Preferably ones that are large enough to see with the naked eye[1]. And they won't have to campaign long, because by about 2015 coins will return in abundance[2]. This will happen in part due to the introduction of a single European currency, originally started in the late 20th century.

Unfortunately, as more and more countries opt into the system, there will be several arguments about the design of the coin, because every country involved (and there'll be lots by then) will want something of *their* country represented on the coin[3]. Naturally every time a new country joins the EU, the whole coin debate will start all over again. The European Parliament, by then established in Iceland, will refuse to allow any country to have its monarch, prime minister or favourite pop

1. Or even the eye that's wearing a natty little pair of tartan trousers.
2. Abundance means plentiful – it doesn't mean doughnuts doing the can-can.
3. A throwback to the Middle Ages when everybody wanted their own coins.

star on the coin and so countries will get more and more devious in their choice of emblem.

Early designs for the coin will feature a frog's leg (France), a sausage (Germany), chips (Belgium), a gondola (Italy), a bullfight (Spain), a pint of stout (Ireland) and a mad cow (Great Britain).

Early trial versions of the coin will be two metres across, and it'll be this more than anything else that causes the most problems[1]. To solve the problem a different coin will be minted each year, featuring a picture of that year's Eurovision Song Contest Winner. Naturally, there'll never be a coin minted in Denmark.

EFFECT

Assuming that your parents have failed to notice that you're in your thirties - and let's face it, it's possible, parents are not big on noticing things - they will probably return to paying your pocket money in cash.

This will effectively end your highly lucrative, electronic banking scam. Of course, if you've overdone the scam your parents could now be living in a

1. There'll be an attempt to put a hole in the middle like Chinese coins, to make the thing light enough to carry. This won't work.

cardboard box in the back garden of your luxury palace, and you might well be paying *them*. Either way the return to coins could be disastrous.

COPING

Point out just how dangerous coins are, even quite large ones. They can get stuck up the hoover (a good reason for not doing the housework!) or jammed in the dog's ear (dogs are stupid enough to let that happen!). Would the *Titanic* have sunk if everyone on board hadn't had their pockets chock-full of very heavy loose change?

Of course it wouldn't! One or other of these arguments might work. If they don't then you'll just have to hope that you invested the profits from your electronic banking scam wisely.

PREDICTION SOURCE

A quick casting of the *runes* (scrabble tiles) spelt the word "ECU a whoppa, but a hat". This was taken by everybody to mean that the ECU (as the European Single Currency coin will be called) was going to be so big that you could wear it on your head. Yes, I know, it seems a bit unlikely, but that's what the runes spelt out. I have to say that we tried every possible combination and that's all we could come up with.

I ventured to suggest that maybe the runes weren't actually trying to tell us anything. Paddy didn't agree. He was convinced that the runes should be taken seriously.

So we all agreed; after all he is an astrologer and probably knows what he's talking about (we based this assumption on Mystic Meg, who always seemed to get the lottery winners right, apparently). Dave also pointed out that, according to Neville, the various countries in the EU have never been able to agree on a coin design. So that clinched it.

While we were interpreting this runic message, Elderado came in to take all our temperatures - which he did every hour. He saw the runes and said, "That's a good idea!", left, and returned later with tea and biscuits. When we questioned him about this he pointed out that the "runes" were clearly spelling *what about a cuppa, eh?* A quick reshuffle proved him to be right. However, we all agreed that the original interpretation should stand. We also all agreed that the tea was totally disgusting. But then it did have a spoonful of Clearosil in it; for our complexions, apparently.

TRAVEL

Governments will be taking steps to reduce the number of cars, etc., on our roads[1]. In order to do this the price of petrol will go up and up. The Petrol Wars will start, with petrol companies offering free gifts to get people to buy their petrol rather than anyone else's.

Things will reach a peak in about 2009 when the McDonald's Petrol Company will offer a free car with

1. Although they won't be doing anything about reducing the amount of chip wrappers, etc., on our roads.

every litre of petrol. KFP (Kentucky Fried Petrol) will try to compete with this by offering you your own personal planet for each full tank. They'll think that they're on to a winner, because they'll naturally assume that you've got no way to *get* to your planet even if you take up their offer. They'll be proved *wrong* – but not yet.

EFFECT

If by now you're thinking of getting your own car, this could be the way to do it. I say *could be* but it's highly unlikely, mainly because your parents will stop you, arguing that since they pay for the petrol, and since petrol costs more than the car, *they* should keep any free gifts.

COPING

Persuade them to buy KFP, thus winning their very own planet. Then offer to help them pack.

PREDICTION SOURCE

Historic. Even in 1998 the Government was talking about ways to reduce traffic and fuel consumption[1].

THE THREE Rs

The coin revolution won't impact on all sections of life. Schools, for instance, will still be caught up in the credit card boom; but then schools are always at least ten years behind the times. Lessons will now be linked to credit. This will work as follows: every time you enter the school building you'll have to "swipe" your card (and wipe your feet). This will give you a "credit" on your card that can be used to pay for lunch, books or even *more* lessons! The more lessons you attend (and

1. These are not necessarily linked, by the way. Fire-eaters regularly swallow petrol by accident, but never when they're in a car. This is because fire-eaters don't believe in drinking and driving.

swipe your lesson credit card for), the more credits you'll get, and the more teaching you'll be given.

This is the Department of Education's (sorry - the People's Getting Cleverer Support Authority's) way of combating truancy, and it won't work. Now obviously you can see why, but then you're cleverer than they are. But I'll explain anyway, just in case: the reason most people bunk off school is to avoid lessons, so offering them a way to earn more lessons is madness. But that won't stop it happening!

EFFECT

More people will bunk off school.

COPING

Lose your school credit card! They won't be able to afford to give you another one. The quickest way to lose it would be to leave it on the school bus, where a First Year will eat it.

COMMUNICATION ☎

The satellite phone - until now a rich person's toy or a TV news crew's lifeline - will become available in high street shops. This is thanks to Japanese technology, which will have miniaturized the phones, previously the size of a large suitcase, to the size of a Mars bar[1]. The only downside is the fact that, to work properly, they have to have their own little satellite dish. But don't worry, wearing one of these on top of your head won't look out of place (see **Fashion** - next).

EFFECT

You should be able to phone absolutely anybody absolutely anywhere with absolutely no problems.

1. Ironically a Mars bar will be the size of a pinhead by then, and cost a million pounds.

Absolutely no problems that is, except the cost!

COPING

Make sure you reverse the charges!

PREDICTION SOURCE

Historic. Since 1877 the telephone has gone from something like this

to something like this

The first version could transmit a message from one room to another along a wire. The second version could transmit a message from one continent to another without any wires, as long as you weren't in a tunnel or didn't have a bucket on your head. It stands to reason therefore that the next stage will be to solve the tunnel thing and increase the range. Having done that, the next problem will be reducing the whole thing. And that's what will take the time.

FASHION

This is the age of digital technology, and fashion will reflect this. You may feel that we're already in the digital age, but you ain't seen nothing yet! Here are just a few examples of what you can expect the best-dressed fashion slaves of the 2010s to be wearing.

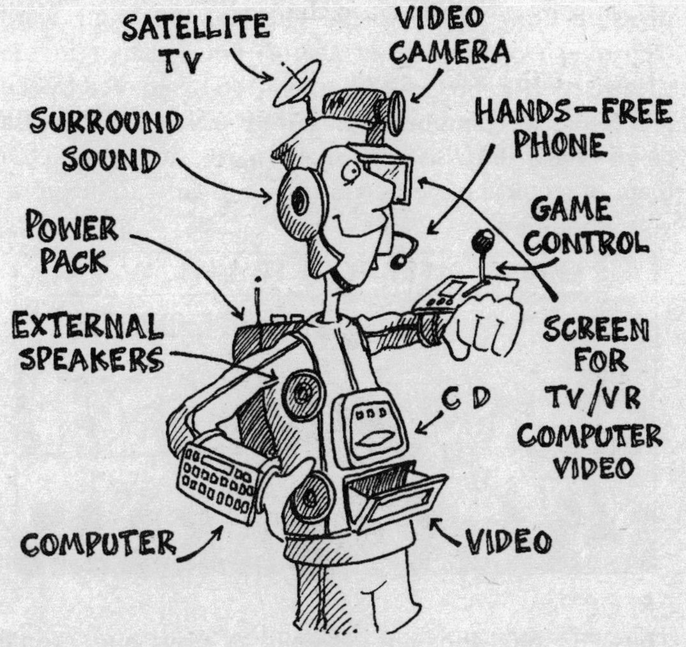

IN: Anything involving microchips.
OUT: Anything involving chips.

MONEY

Despite all efforts to make hospitals cost-effective, the Health Service is still not working. A plan to replace hospitals with the Greek *aesculapia* is unveiled. Patients will book themselves in for a week or a fortnight while doctors discover what diseases they have, ignore the old ones and write books about the new ones. The whole thing will be run rather on the lines of the holiday camps that were so popular throughout the middle bit of the

20th century. A typical first night at hospital - renamed *Hospital Inns* - will involve a Meet 'n' Greet, which replaces the old-fashioned medical check-in (blood pressure etc.). Once you've checked into your ward (renamed *Dormitories of Dettol*) you'll gather in the theatre (performing, not operating) to be greeted by the MC (medical communicator). After which you'll play a game of *Whose Disease is it Anyway*?, during which a team of medical experts will try - and fail - to diagnose your condition.

EFFECT

These Hospital Inns are designed as a rest cure. You'll get neither. However, you will leave there several pounds lighter. Several *hundred* pounds lighter, in fact!

COPING

Try and stay healthy (see **Leisure** - next).

LEISURE / SPORT

Every now and again the world goes on a huge fitness kick, usually started by the Americans. Nearly two decades of sitting in front of computers, plus the fact that home shopping will have replaced the weekly trip to the supermarket, will mean that most developed countries will be full of extremely unfit people. A group of scientists who have run out of diseases to discover will turn their attention to the world's health. After all, there's got to be several books in it, if not a video.

EFFECT

We'll all be a lot fitter. Possibly. We'll certainly be made to feel a lot guiltier if we don't make an effort.

COPING

Go with the flow and exercise. Or go into a cupboard and hide. This health kick is a passing phase. It'll only last six years.

PREDICTION SOURCE

Neville the psychic cockle. Somehow he escaped from his paddling pool and was found clinging to a pair of jogging bottoms, having left a slimy trail all the way up one leg. "It's a sign!" claimed Dave Dilks. "It looks more like a stain to me," I said. But I was outvoted.

EXPLORATION

I expect a lot of you want to know whether or not life will be found on other planets. I put this to the team and they threw everything they could at the problem: buns, shaving foam, next door's goat. Eventually we realized that we weren't getting anywhere, and so we gave the tarot cards a try. Not the ones in Neville's pool. Frankly, you'd have to have had enough tetanus injections to immunize an entire army, and even then you wouldn't want to put so much as the tip of one hair on your head[1] into that water.

So we sent Elderado out to the local Pork Sausage and

1. Or any other part of your body for that matter.

Tarot Card Shop (every town has one) to buy a deck. He was gone for hours, mainly because he stopped at the local post office to give a row of pensioners a complete medical. They were delighted. Most of them had only come in to buy a stamp[1].

The last thing they expected (or dared hope for) was a complete medical conducted, in broad daylight, by *the* Florence Nightingale. On his return we got down to business.

Now the mysteries of the tarot are exactly that as far as I'm concerned. So who am I to argue with the interpretation offered by Mrs Wibley, who was so good she could even read tea bags? She can just look into your empty cup and say, "I bet you'll be wanting another one!" Amazing! How does she do it? I was less impressed, I have to say, by her tarot reading. "Well, dear," she said to an elk who had wandered in out of the rain, "I don't know about outer space, but according to these cards, life will be discovered in Basingstoke." And do you know what? The very next day it was. Not life as we know it, but life anyway.

EFFECT

Scary.

COPING

Avoid Basingstoke.

1. Why it should take 25 old people to buy one stamp defeats me.

LIFESTYLE

Technology will obviously impact on our general lifestyle, the things we eat, for instance. If you are sent shopping you'll no longer have to worry about checking whether things are past their sell-by date. When you reach the checkout the computerized scanning system will automatically do this for you. Of course, it'll still be your choice whether or not you want to take a chance and buy the stuff. If you do the computer will go "You'll be sorry!" in a silly whiny voice.

EFFECT

This could be a good thing as it will prevent you from getting food poisoning. That's the theory anyway. The downside is that you'll have to follow the advice of a computer.

COPING

Listen to the computer – if you can bear it.

PREDICTION SOURCE

Historic. In about 1996 someone invented a machine that read barcodes and could tell you what additives were in various food products. The logical step would be an ability to read sell-by dates. Ah, that's a point! Are these things *ever* logical?

2021–2030

During this period you'll probably be nudging forty-something. At some point during this decade you'll get a birthday card with a giant badge on it saying: "Oh no! 4–0!"[1] As if that's not bad enough, you'll think it's *really funny*! Don't get upset – life gets worse! You may have children by now. They may even be teenagers. You'll probably find yourself saying things like "I didn't do that when I was your age!" Stop! Think back! You did, you know!

And you didn't think it was so wrong then, so why is it now? And all the time the world about you will be changing. For example...

MONEY

Hopefully you *will* have invested your money (OK – your *parent's* money!) wisely – but equally hopefully not in plastic. Because, due to the overuse of credit and other cards, and also to the lack of natural resources on the planet, there will now be a world shortage of materials used in the production of plastic.

EFFECT

Cards will be recalled and pulped to make new ones; but only for the super rich.

1. Yes! This sort of thing will still exist in 20 or so years' time!

COPING

If your electronic banking scam worked, then you've got nothing to fear because you will be one of the super rich. If not, then ignore the advice I gave you ten years ago, and start convincing your parents to pay your pocket money in coins. You should easily be able to do this, because if you're still conning your mum and dad out of pocket money by the 2020s, then you're capable of absolutely anything!

TRAVEL

A major breakthrough – the solar car! Yes, I know that these have been around since the 1990s, but this is one that actually works and can be mass-produced. Just as the mass-produced Model T Ford revolutionized car travel in 1908, this will go some way to solving the fuel shortage. But before you get too excited there will be a drawback. The best models will still be outrageously expensive; far too expensive for most families[1]. However, there will be cheaper models. The *Lunalada*, for example, will be very cheap indeed. Unfortunately it'll turn out to be badly named, as it won't work in the dark!

EFFECT

To revolutionize car travel, but only for a few. The rest of us will probably be walking everywhere by now, anyway.

1. Especially if your parents have lost all their cash to you in pocket money!

COPING

Cultivate rich friends. This is probably a good idea anyway!

THE THREE Rs

One word will symbolize the education revolution of the 2020s. And that word is ... semolina. No, it isn't! It's *computers.* This may strike you as being obvious. You may in fact have expected this to happen much earlier. After all, a lot of schools were already connected to the Internet in the late 1990s, and computer software was an accepted learning tool[1]. But the goal by the end of this second ten-year period will be to make sure that every child in every school has their very own school computer. Not one on a trolley that gets wheeled around the school, or even ten in a room that you need special permission to access – but one *each.*

EFFECT

Teachers will be huffy (OK – *more* huffy!). This is because they don't like lots of computers in the classroom, partly because they take up valuable teacher space, but more especially because they *still* won't know how to use them. The problem for you will be bearing the brunt of the teacher's huffiness.

1. In fact, the Government's goal for 2002 was for 50% of all schoolchildren to have an e-mail address, and virtual teaching existed on the Internet.

COPING

Be nice to teacher/college lecturer. Make sure you do all your homework. It won't work but do it anyway!

PREDICTION SOURCE

This was according to Nostradamus. During a particularly heavy Ouija board session, where the glass shot off the table several times, soaking my trousers (I told Elderado that it wasn't supposed to have Coke in it but he wouldn't listen), Nostradamus revealed to us that "the learned one will rage as the child seeks the glass of knowledge". After a bit of debate we took this to mean that teachers would feel very left out because students were getting all the information from a computer screen (*glass of knowledge*).

This seemed to be borne out by the fact that the Government had said that they were committed to providing computers for all pupils. In fact, Nostradamus didn't mean any such thing. He was actually talking about somebody's mum getting cross about them watching too much television.

COMMUNICATION

The videophone will be in common use. This had been around since the mid-1980s, but had never really caught on in a big way[1]. There are a few reasons for this: one is

1. Jeremy Beadle had one, so that just shows you how unpopular it was!

that it was always too expensive. But the main reason is that most of us don't really want to look at the person we're talking to, even in real life, so why would we want to do it over the phone? Imagine, if you can, having to phone your school to tell the lady in the office that you were at death's door so couldn't come in, when all the time she could look at you and see that you were the picture of health.

But far, far worse than this – imagine having to look at *her ugly face*!

EFFECT

Anyone you phone will be able to see you, and vice versa.

COPING

Stick a bag on your head and only phone beautiful people.

PREDICTION SOURCE

Paddy O'Dors. One day he spent the whole morning drawing up an astral chart. We were fascinated, trying to imagine what deep insight this was going to provide into the future. After all, it just looked like a series of squiggles to the untrained eye[1]. A child of three could

1. It would probably even look like squiggles to an eye with years of training, plus a black belt in karate.

have done it with their arms tied behind their back. Well, one arm, anyway. Through a silence that you could have cut with the side of a bit of paper came this gem of astral insight: "I bet everyone will have a videophone one day." Unbelievable! Could he really tell that from one sideways glance at these squiggles? Well, no actually. He wasn't even looking at the squiggles. He was just thinking aloud. But he's probably right.

FASHION

Hey! If people are going to be able to see you on the phone, fashion just has to reflect this. Here's how the catwalk will cope!

IN: Face masks.
OUT: Zits. Although most people will still have them.

MEDICINE

I think it was Jesus who said, "If thine eye offends thee, pluck it out!" To which everyone replied, "After you, matey!" But this is where medicine will be by the mid-

2020s. You've heard of hormone replacement? No? Well, basically it's when they replace your hormones. All right now? Anyway, this will lead to *body part* replacement. Advanced transplant surgery.

"Hang on!" you're saying. "We've already got that!" True. We've got transplant surgery. This is *advanced* transplant surgery. Using the limbs and organs of other animals. It was already being considered in the 1990s. Pigs' livers were considered. A test programme was even set up. It was a bit of a failure, mainly because the surgeons were lightly braising the livers and adding onions before transplant. The patients never went hungry again. Unfortunately they never went home again, either.

Not in the least put off by this disaster, surgeons have continued to develop the process, until by the end of this decade it will be perfectly possible to transplant any part of any animal to any human being. It won't have much practical application in genuine medicine, but since hospitals will be glorified hotels by then, it won't matter. No! The big market will be in *cosmetic* surgery! Imagine the potential: always late for the bus? Then have your legs replaced with those of a greyhound. You'll never miss that bus again - unless, of course, a rabbit runs past.

EFFECT

There'll be some very odd-looking people about. Videophone calls should become very interesting!

COPING

Don't consider this kind of surgery for a second, or even less. What looks great on a water buffalo might not suit you at all.

LEISURE / SPORT

After considerable pressure from the Countryside Lobby, now renamed The People's Looking After Trees and Stuff Lobby, the Powers That Be will finally pass a law banning the hunting of smokers with dogs. Or should that read the hunting – with dogs – of smokers? People with dogs will no longer be allowed to hunt smokers, anyway. This will be a great relief for everyone, not least of all the dogs themselves, many of whom are beagles and as such are ex-smokers[1]. This could mark a reversal in people's attitudes towards smoking. Our research suggests that the practice, by restaurants, of shooting 50,000 volts of electricity up through the chairs of anybody who dares to light up could also be banned, although this is unlikely. After all, this is the only form of entertainment many restaurants in this decade will be able to afford to provide.

1. From their days working in research centres.

EFFECT

Anyone and everyone will be able to smoke without fear of hearing a haunting sound of a hunting horn and seeing men in red coats coming through the lounge window on horseback. However, death from smoking is much more lingering and horrible than being mown down by the Lincolnshire Hunt.

COPING

It's safer not to smoke in the first place!

PREDICTION SOURCE

A dream I had. It's that simple!

EXPLORATION

It had to happen. No, I'm not talking about *You've Been Framed* being taken off the telly, although that's long overdue. I'm actually talking about virtual space travel. Anyone with a virtual reality helmet, access to the Internet and a geeky nature will be able to prance about on the surface of Jupiter without even leaving their bedroom – or anyone else's bedroom for that matter.

So how will it work? Well, according to my science expert – actually Mrs Wibley's son Trevor, who once bought a copy of *Science Monthly* and now considers himself a world authority on such matters – satellite shots of Jupiter (and other planets) will be beamed to a website near you and then you will be able to immerse yourself in them via your VR helmet. Now you may imagine that this should have happened much sooner, given that VR technology was quite advanced even in the late 20th century. Well, yes. But the reason this wasn't available sooner is that not enough planets had been explored. After all, this is not going to be cheap, and so people need to be offered as many planets as possible. The technicians behind this will probably make a few up as well.

EFFECT

You will have the feeling that you are walking on another planet. It will be so realistic that you'll probably suffer from gravity sickness and throw up all over your Star Trek duvet. Your mum will be over the Moon[1]!

EFFECT

Wait for the real thing. It has to come – and soon!

PREDICTION SOURCE

Trevor Wibley – science expert and double-glazing salesman.

LIFESTYLE

The technological tentacles of the Computer Age will also be felt in the high street. That's almost poetic, isn't it? OK, so I'm no Ted Hughes[2] (bloke who's written

1. Not!
2. If Ted Hughes had written that sentence, it would have a dead animal in it somewhere.

loads of poetry), but it's not bad. But what does it mean? Well, it basically means that shops will be computerized as well. But don't worry, computers won't replace shop assistants. After all, how can something as sophisticated and complex as a computer be expected to stand there going "I don't know" to everything you ask it? And this, as you probably know, is an important part of the psychology of shopping.

It works like this: you go into a shop not at all sure whether a) you really want to buy the thing you've gone in to buy, or b) whether you can actually afford it, or even c) whether your parents will go totally ape when you get it home. But, after ten minutes of the shop assistant saying "I don't know", you are so desperate to buy said item that you would kill for it – or at least pay well over the odds for it.

But where do the computers come in?, I hear you think[1]. I'll tell you: once the assistant has got you hooked on buying the thing he or she will point to the computer and say, "My colleague will take your money." They think the computer's a person, for Heaven's sake! Mind you, it is wearing a little paper hat. The computer will then "process" the sale. By which I mean that it will instruct you to "swipe" your credit card. It will then take your "purchase", swap it for one with a dirty mark

1. Or at least I *think* I hear you think. I think.

on it, and wrap it before you notice; informing you in a very polite (if robotic) voice that "Purchases cannot be exchanged or money refunded. Have a nice day."

Robotic. Robots. That's something I've not mentioned, and already it's the 2020s. Well, imagine if you will that when I talk of computers I'm referring to anything computerized, some of which will be robots and resemble humans. In fact, some of them will be more human than real humans. But then I expect we all know people who make us realize that in many cases this won't be particularly difficult.

EFFECT

Shopping will be "more efficient" – i.e. take a lot longer.

COPING

Go up to the computer and say, "Can I speak to the manager, please?" This is just one of the questions that it won't be programmed to answer.

2031-2040

During this decade you'll be about fifty[1]. And you thought you'd never make it past 25! It's amazing that – at 15 – 50 seems so very *old*, doesn't it? And yet here you are – and you don't *feel* old, whatever old feels like. Obviously your kids will think you're old, but then what do they know? Probably more than you knew at their age. But then the world has changed so much; or has it? For instance…

MONEY

World currency is in a state of flux. All natural resources are in short supply, and therefore coins and plastic credit cards disappear. However, due to a sharp change in world climate there is an explosion in the world gerbil and other fluffy animal populations, and therefore gerbils etc. become the new world currency. This presents a few problems: nobody can put their hand in their pocket to get out their "money" without it biting them; "money" becomes extremely difficult to transport in large quantities. You also have to feed it. Due to shortage of materials and a failure to agree on anything, the European Single Currency disappears and is replaced by a range of currencies. Exchange rates return and a typical exchange rate board will now look like this:

2·5 UK GERBILS = 1·02 US POLECATS

2·0 UK GERBILS = 2·47 AUS KANGAROOS

3·0 UK GERBILS = 7·05 FRA FROGS

1. If you're reading this book in 1999.

EFFECT

You'll refuse pocket money (assuming that you can still get it) because it stinks your room out!

COPING

Roll with it. I can't see this lasting. After all, it would only take the entire lemming population to throw themselves off a cliff, and the economy of somewhere like Belgium would completely collapse.

PREDICTION SOURCE

Paddy O'Dors, who was starting to feel a bit left out in the prediction stakes. Nobody's fault exactly, it's just that it takes much longer to prepare an astral chart than it does to throw a few runes (sorry - *Scrabble* tiles). Anyway, according to Paddy in the 2030s (June 2034 to be more precise) there will be a strong link between small furry animals and money. We spent a long time trying to assess what this link would be; Mrs W suggested that perhaps it meant that our pets would all have their own bank accounts, but that just seemed too far fetched to even consider. No, pets as pocket money seemed a far more reasonable notion.

TRAVEL

With the introduction of virtual travel, the need to actually pack up the car, and put up with younger brothers being sick and saying, "Are we nearly there yet?" will completely disappear. Even the sight of hundreds of people sitting around - totally stranded - at an airport, will become a thing of the past. After all, if we can visit a virtual Venus, why not do the same thing with Skegness? The advantage that the virtual Skeggy would have over the real thing would be the smell of dead fish; the virtual one would have to have it added on afterwards.

EFFECT

Visiting a virtual resort should help you decide whether or not you want to go to the real one. If it's a really cool place it might help persuade parents to take their children, *before* they get a chance to check the price! On the other hand, if parents experience the resort before they go there, they'll probably say, "We don't need to bother going there now!" But then that's parents for you.

COPING

Virtual travel will be an exciting thing, not to mention a useful learning tool. Just keep it away from adults! (Unless you're one yourself by now!)

PREDICTION SOURCE

Trevor Wibley again. Fortunately, shortly after this he got a call on his video mobile to tell him that the windows had just fallen out of his own flat. Serves him right for getting his own company to fit them! Ho ho!

Computers will have completely replaced teachers in the classroom by the mid 2030s. So what will teachers be doing? The only thing that they are properly trained for – they'll become Professional Sarcastics. They'll be employed in clothes shops to say to customers "Oh yes! You look really good in that!" in a way that will make the customer feel about two inches tall. At the moment this is done by the shop assistants themselves, but frankly they don't have the training or skill to handle *real* sarcasm and so it just comes out as unpleasantness[1]. The only problem that teachers will have with this is their own appalling dress sense. Teachers have no fashion sense whatsoever. They can't even brush their hair properly. Customers will therefore be unlikely to feel intimidated by the sarcasm of someone who looks like they've had a huge electric shock while ram-raiding Oxfam.

To get around this, the shops will put the teachers inside large cardboard boxes with a picture of the latest supermodel on the side. Amazingly – probably because of the pathetic lighting in most clothes stores – this will fool *everybody*.

1. I'm not suggesting that some teachers aren't unpleasant. Far from it! Most of them can be unpleasant to Olympic standards.

EFFECT

Once you catch on to the fact that your ex-maths teacher is now the regular Sarcastic in Clothes-4-U in the high street, you'll naturally want to pop along to point and snigger. This novelty will soon wear off, however, as you witness firsthand something you had mercifully forgotten: the fact that your ex-teacher's biting sarcasm can reduce even the thickest skin to a blubbering jelly.

COPING

As you pass your ex-teacher inside their cardboard "fashion suit" say: "You look nice, sir!" Teachers respond with doglike loyalty to anyone who is nice to them; mainly because nobody ever is!

PREDICTION SOURCE

Historic. In fact - due to poor pay - many teachers are already working in clothes shops at weekends, just after they finish their milk round.

COMMUNICATION ☎

You may be thinking, "If the number of phones increases (which they will), and if the number of computers connected to phone-lines increases (which they will as well), then aren't we eventually going to run out of phone-lines?" Yes. We are. But - and it's a big but. Well no it isn't.

That's a big but.

But those clever people who organize phone-lines and stuff are on the case, even as we speak. They're not just sitting around inventing more and more telephone services (*Call Waiting, Call Divert, Talk to Yourself Nobody Else is Listening,* etc.), oh no! They are also looking into ways of increasing the number of available lines. They'll do this by three methods: firstly, they'll improve the cables that they use to transmit telephone calls; secondly, they'll increase the number of satellites that you can "bounce" calls off; and thirdly they'll increase the number of available numbers. How will they do this? By adding an extra digit; they did this in April 1995, by adding a "1" to all phone area codes, making the number 01-something. And then they'll do this again; and again; and again.

In fact by the end of this current decade (2040) the average phone number will be so long that it will be quicker to travel to, say, Australia, than it will be to dial it. But do you think it'll stop there? Yes? Think again! Eventually phone numbers will be so long that they'll have to introduce letters and even little pictures to relieve the monotony. Our research suggested that, by 2040, my phone number will be 010980938-6GHJUYT3564137KU906HFJA ?? 5348364GOC7 ?????-???? 623548V2 B7038-N8. Don't bother calling me, just in case I'm not in!

EFFECT

A lot of finger ache.

COPING

Use e-mail!

FASHION

Fashion will reflect the change in currency and the introduction of virtual travel. Here's just a few examples of what the smartly dressed Child of the Twothousandandforties will be wearing:

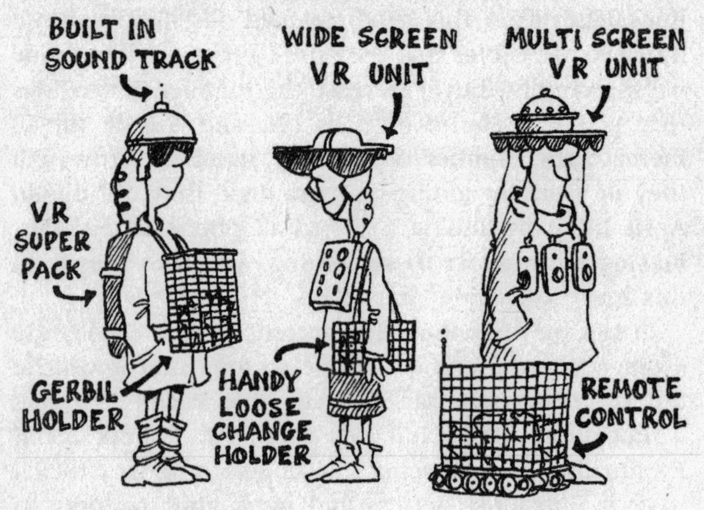

IN: Anything VR.
OUT: Phoning people!

MEDICINE

They swore it would never happen! But it will; about now. I'm talking 'bout cloning. Cloning of animals will already be up and running as the world panics about food shortages. And naturally once everyone gets used to the idea of cloning animals, the idea of cloning humans will be just *one small step for mankind*. The idea may make you want to go AGH!!!!, so feel free. I'm happy to wait. No, in fact I'll join you:

AGHHHHH!!!!!!

That's better. But now, let's consider the benefits. Suppose there were two of you. One of you could be out playing while the other did your homework. You could two-time your girl/boyfriend without them ever finding out. You could even go out with somebody long after you'd packed them in. There are loads of other benefits (any identical twin will probably give you the full list). The problem is probably going to be deciding which of you does the rubbish job while the other has the fun.

EFFECT

A lot of confusion as people try and work out whether it's *déjà vu*, cloning or double vision.

COPING

Avoid it! After all, you are unique! Both of you!

PREDICTION SOURCE

Historic. Our sources tell us that Saddam Hussein had already been cloned in 1998. Why else would he have needed 14 palaces?

LEISURE/SPORT

Naturally, if cloning does take off as my team is predicting, then it could have a big impact on sport. Imagine a star player being cloned 11 times so that he can play in every position. Brilliant! The only problem is that if he was sent off, then the whole team would go off[1]!

EXPLORATION

For the time being, people will be happy with virtual space travel. After all, there are other things to think about – avoiding getting cloned in your sleep for a start! What a dreadful thought! Your mum might wake the wrong person up! Meanwhile, scientists will be exploring the oceans, looking for alternative foods, fuels, or even just a big wreck to make a film about.

EFFECT

We could be living on fish for the rest of our lives. Worse still, we could all be driving fish-fuelled cars!

COPING

Get in huge stocks of tinned food!

1. The other problem with cloning footballers is that they'd all have to share a brain cell.

LIFESTYLE

The disturbing thing during this decade is that – if you're 50 – you'll probably find yourself worrying about the characters in *Emmerdale* – now in it's 65th year, and now called *Up North*. Gosh, hasn't it developed since you used to avoid watching it as a child? First it was called *Emmerdale Farm*, and was about a farm, then it became *Emmerdale* and was about the whole village, and now it's about the whole of the north of England, which by then will have its own parliament.

PREDICTION SOURCE

The *TV Times*!

EFFECT

You'll try to avoid worrying about *Emmerdale*, just as you'll try not to feel sorry for Bianca in *EastEnders*, now 60 and living on her own. This is because Ricky (sorry – "Riiiccccckkkkyyyy!!!!") will get abducted by aliens (in a particularly believable story-line), and she's left to run their pig farm on her own. Pig farm? Yes! Sorry, didn't you know? Albert Square gets turned into an inner city farming community.

COPING

Although you may panic at first that you've become as obsessed with soaps as your parents are, don't worry. Pretty soon you'll bump into some old school pals and realize that they're afflicted too. It's normal!

PREDICTION SOURCE

Historic. The TV digital revolution has had the effect of forcing TV companies to make more of the same stuff, and repeat things. Hardly a revolution at all, really!

2041 - 2050

60! Or there about. The birthdays aren't harder to handle, they're just harder to remember. Not because your brain's going, but because the world about you is changing almost daily. For instance...

MONEY

You could be drawing your state pension. Except for the fact that state pensions will no longer exist, replaced some years earlier by the People's Right to Be Old Enough To Give Up Work Allowance. This is exactly the same as the state pension, except for the name; and the size. Because of the rate of inflation pensions will have grown from 25p in 1909 to a massive £75,000 - or 36 gerbils - by 2050. But before you get excited I should point out that a loaf of bread will cost 52 gerbils[1].

EFFECT

The pound, gerbil or even hole in your pocket will be worth a lot more than in previous years. Unfortunately, everything else will have gone up as well.

COPING

Spend it while you've got it. Don't bother to put any cash aside for a rainy day, because global warming will

1. Or would if gerbils hadn't been replaced by coins.

mean that rainy days hardly ever happen!

TRAVEL

Or more precisely *space* travel! Yes! The *real* thing, not some virtual experience. Well, it had to happen eventually. The first men walked on the Moon in 1969, but since then – what? Plenty of books, films and the like; plenty of pictures of moon rock and Mars dust – not to mention Saturn fluff probably – but no blokes in silly suits walking in a very strange way. Well, that will be put right in the middle of this decade. If you fancy going to Venus, Pluto or even Uranus, all you'll need to do is pack a bag, go to the Space Travel Terminal, board a shuttle, and six to 12 months later you'll be lying on a purple beach sipping something that looks (and tastes) like brake fluid.

Six to 12 MONTHS! Well, yes, but after all we're talking long distance travel here. Some people wait up to four months in an airport departure lounge just to fly to Benidorm, so I don't think 12 months is a long time to wait to go to another planet. But I know what you're thinking. You're thinking, "How about if I change my mind while I'm travelling there?" or "How about if we get a couple of months into the flight and I can't remember if I've turned the tap off properly? Or fed the fish?[1]". These are reasonable fears. But unfortunately you won't be able to do anything about them.

1. Don't worry about the fish. The Earth will probably be so radioactive by then that the fish will mutate long before they die of starvation.

EFFECT

We'll have a wider choice of holiday destination. And because it'll take so long to get there - and cost so much - we'll only need a holiday every five years!

COPING

Persuade whoever is making the decisions about where you go on holiday by this time, that Margate's quite nice. It's certainly got more amusement arcades than the Moon, anyway.

PREDICTION SOURCE

Paddy O'Dors. Whilst studying the heavens through his extremely powerful telescope he thought he saw a family of five picnicking beside the Sea of Tranquillity. It turned out to be the rotting remains of a family of flies who'd somehow met their untimely end on the end of his telescope. We gave them a decent burial - well, washed them down the sink anyway. But Paddy was sure that this was a sign.

"Yes," agreed Mrs Wibley. "It's a sign that the double glazing isn't working properly!" Then turning to me with a superior expression she said, "If my Trevor had fitted your windows your house would be a fly-free zone." I didn't like to point out that her Trevor was currently round at his own flat where *his* windows were lying all over the road outside. I didn't like to but I did point it out. Boy, did she get a crinkly mouth, which Elderado immediately treated with Crinkly Mouth Cream.

But Paddy was adamant. This was a sign. A sign that people (and flies maybe) would eventually live happily ever after on other planets. Who am I to argue? Well actually I would have done, except for the fact that Elderado had recently put me on the latest Hollywood fad, *Kate Winslet's Prune & Fig Diet,* and so I had to rush away unexpectedly. However, it is fair to say that one day we will fly to other planets, so why not in the 2040s?

THE THREE Rs

Computerized teaching will come under fire, worst luck! This is mainly because computers are not very good at setting and collecting homework. Now you probably think that this is a really good thing, but it's unlikely that parents would agree. You see, the fact of you (as a child) having no homework effectively halves the number of things that parents can criticize you for, and as we all know parents do like to criticize. So teachers will be brought in to do the menial tasks, such as setting homework, collecting it in, moaning that it's late, forgetting to mark it, etc.

They may even have to run detentions, although they won't be allowed to give them out. This is a pity because computers will get the whole detention thing completely wrong; being a machine they won't be able to tell who is actually causing trouble, and so they'll just give *everyone* a detention. Oh – no change from real teachers really!

EFFECT

Although pupils will be strangely relieved to see a teacher in class again, they'll quickly realize that this is not a return to the good old days when a teacher's job was to keep you under control and your job was to make that as tricky as possible. In fact, it'll soon become obvious that the teacher is as much a victim of the system as the pupils are. You'll even find yourself feeling sorry for "Sir" (or "Miss"). You may find this impossible to accept now, but it'll happen, believe me.

COPING

Resist all temptation to feel sorry for your teacher. After all, who taught the people who invented the computers that took over teaching you and made your life a misery? That's right – teachers. I rest my case.

COMMUNICATION ☎

A rapidly clogging Internet and infeasibly long telephone numbers will cause us to look for alternative methods of communication. Laws banning unnecessary use of the phone will be brought in.

It'll become illegal, for instance, to phone somebody in the same room; although phoning someone in the same *house* will still be OK, as long as you don't contact Directory Enquiries to get the number. Obviously, this will cause a backlash. People will say that it's an infringement of their human rights not to be allowed to phone whoever they want, *wherever* they want. The Countrywide Phone Lobby will march on parliament, now relocated in the Millennium Dome. Unfortunately, everyone they need to speak to will be on the phone.

EFFECT

We'll all have to think really carefully about whether or not we actually need to make a particular call. While we're trying to sort this out, we'll probably contact the person by Internet instead.

COPING

Sit tight. If people want to talk, they'll call *you*. Although they might not.

PREDICTION SOURCE

Mrs Wibley. But not, I have to admit, as the result of a seance or any nifty bit of rune casting. She just happened to say, over a cup of home-made lentil and rhubarb soup, "Have you noticed that everybody you phone these days is engaged?" There was some confusion at first. We all thought she was talking about marriage, mainly because she usually is. She's desperate to get her Trevor married to somebody. She thinks he would be a real catch. She's totally wrong. But she's right about the phones.

FASHION

There's always a period of history to which people look back and say, "Did people *really* go around looking like *that*?!?" And this is it! Yes, just as the sixties of the 20th century were a period of fashion lunacy, so the 2040s will earn their own special place in the wastebasket of fashion history. Here's a snapshot of the sort of things you can expect. Prepare to shudder!

IN: Anything stupid.
OUT: Anything sensible.

MEDICINE

The desire by doctors to keep people alive as long as possible will never be stronger than in the 2040s. After all, doctors will argue, our patients have made it half-way through the century (almost), why shouldn't they make it all the way? This will prove to be a crafty way of covering up the fact that doctors no longer have any ideas about how to cure the new diseases that will almost certainly have appeared during the 21st century. Diseases which, to be honest, the doctors invented themselves. What was once "only a rash", or "just a virus" will now have proper medical names.

Or rather they'll bear the name of the doctor who first thought of naming that particular disease. Obviously these names will be dressed up a bit to make them sound impressive. *Pilkington's Pimple* will be one. This will be a totally harmless pimple, usually on the side of the right index finger, brought about by gripping your biro too tight.

New football supporting diseases will also emerge. *Everet's Supporter's Buttock* is what used to be called a sore bottom, but once Dr Wayne Everet gets his hands on it (not literally, obviously!) it'll get a fancy name[1]. This condition will be brought on by watching Manchester City play, as will *Dawson's Goal-less Yawn*.

EFFECT

This will be twofold. On the one hand you'll feel important, knowing that the harmless little spot you have on the end of your nose has a big impressive name. On the other hand, that big impressive name will make you start to worry that maybe the harmless little pimple isn't harmless at all.

COPING

It *is*! Don't worry! On the other hand ... er ... it might not be, er ... oh dear...

LEISURE / SPORT

Talking of sporting injuries, which we weren't, the 2040s will mark a complete change in the nature and number of injuries sustained on the sports field. This will be brought about by a change in the rules of soccer, caused by the seemingly unstoppable rise in violence outside football matches. Violence inside the stadiums was of course greatly reduced by the introduction of all-seater stadiums in the late 1990s. This was mainly due to the fact that, if you want to get at a "fan" from the

1. Incidentally the Latin name will be Everum Supportum Bum.

opposing team, you had to ask everyone in your row to stand up so that you could get past. You'll know how embarrassing this can be in the cinema, and nothing takes the edge off a good punch-up quicker than being embarrassed.

Anyway, to get back to the rule change, which will be: two teams of eleven players will take to the field, one team at each end. After kicking a ball around for a few practice minutes, the referee will toss a coin. The teams will call, and whoever wins the toss will decide which way they play. Once this is decided, the teams will leave the field and lock themselves into a reinforced concrete "bunker". The teams' fans will then take to the field, one lot at each end (the supporters of the team who won the toss get to choose which end they start from). The referee will then blow a whistle and run for cover, as the two lots of supporters battle it out – to the death and beyond probably. The winning side will be the one with the most supporters left alive when the police turn up.

EFFECT

Well, this rather depends on whether you're a fan or a player; or a ref who doesn't get out of the way quick enough. Or whether you just like fighting.

COPING

Stay at home and watch it on TV. It's much safer!

EXPLORATION

Scientists will be twiddling their thumbs, wondering what to do next. After all they can now get a shuttle to the Moon in nine months, and a first-class letter to Carlisle in 12 years: what more is there to explore? This will prove to be the calm before the storm. Exploration of space and this planet will reach new heights in the second half of the 21st century.

EFFECT

Well, who can say? If the whole universe is suddenly going to open up, then who knows what's out there – apart from the truth; at least it is according to the *X-Files*.

COPING

This depends on what you're going to have to cope with. That reinforced concrete football bunker sounds like a good idea!

PREDICTION

Nostradamus – who else? His prediction reads: "Man will travel to other planets and meet alien life-forms". Well, you can't say fairer than that, can you? And even though we all felt that it didn't sound like a typical Nostradamus prediction, because usually you can't understand a word he says, we had to agree that it was a relief that at last we knew what he was talking about. Probably.

LIFESTYLE

Technological breakthroughs lead to faster lifestyles. And the faster they get, the less time there is for things like food. Scientists will be working towards foods that don't need preparing – or even eating. We already have fast food, but this would be completely different. It would be more like astronaut's food; small pills that are actually a three-course candlelit dinner for two.

OK, so it may take the romance out of going to a restaurant, but who said that there were going to be any restaurants by the 2040s? After all, if there are still going to be restaurants, where are they going to build all those car parks?

EFFECT

Well, we've already talked about eating out. But the repercussions are even greater. If you're at school in the

2040s you won't be able to use the old excuse "I'm eating my tea" to get you out of doing your homework. Eating tea will be like taking an aspirin; or it might even be injected into you while you sleep. Worse still, there'll be no more cake adverts on TV, mainly because there'll be no more cakes.

COPING

How will you cope with *that*? How will *anybody*? You'll just have to hope that I've got it wrong!

PREDICTION SOURCE

Neville the psychic cockle. This turned out to be his most important, but last, prediction. It is ironic that it happened to be about food (see next section).

The mists of time – the fog of the future

And talking of getting it wrong, it was at this point in the process that things started to go pear-shaped. I could see that my team were beginning to flag. Every seance left Mrs Wibley with a worse headache; one which could not be relieved even by liberal applications of Parson's Pickle Liniment[1], prepared with Crimean precision by Elderado, who was still in the throes of believing himself to be Florence Nightingale.

Paddy O'Dors had made so many astral charts that he became completely wrapped up in his work – literally! It took several hours to unravel him.

But the worst was yet to come. During a particularly heated discussion about food, ending in the prediction seen above (under **Lifestyle**), Dave Dilks absent-mindedly took out a pin and removed poor Neville from his shell.

1. Which tastes better than it looks, which isn't difficult.

It wasn't until he'd eaten him that he realized what had happened. As you can imagine we were all greatly distressed. It didn't help when Dave belched and commented that Neville "didn't taste any better than he looked". Elderado called Dave a cannibal, which was hardly fair but it made us all feel a lot better.

So the team was one short. We decided to soldier on. But disaster struck again. There's an old proverb: "Disaster is like a bus. It always comes in threes." And so it was with us; first Mrs Wibley's headaches, then Paddy's wind-up, then the death of poor Neville, and now ... oh! Hang on! This'll be four things! Oh well, that's one old proverb out of the window! Anyway, this fourth disaster frankly put the tin hat on things. We were trying to contact Nostradamus, when we got the following psychic message through the ether of past generations: "The number you are calling has not been recognized." And that was it! The last we ever heard of him!

A stranger returns

And that would have been it - the end of our predictions. The book would have been retitled *Coping With The First Half of The 21st Century*. It wouldn't have been any cheaper, obviously, but it would have been shorter. If it hadn't been for the timely arrival of old school "chum[1]" Michael "Call me Mickey" Shorthouse. Yes! My bestest[2] pal was back. And he'd brought a book.

You may not think that this is so unusual, at least not until I tell you that Mickey was never big on books; not a keen reader. Oh yes, he got through all the *Mr Men* books at secondary school, which impressed the rest of us because we hadn't even considered *looking* at the classics. But this book he had with him wasn't his favourite *Mr Bump goes to the Job Centre*. It was *Old Scroat's Almanac*. Now, if you're not familiar with the book, let me just tell you that - when it comes to predicting the future - *Old Scroat's* is *the* definitive work on the subject.

"Mickey - you are brilliant!" I exclaimed, jumping for Joy, who was just trying to make off with the silverware; a rugby tackle will always foil a burglar, even a female one.

I could have kissed Mickey, but then I remembered that we were in mixed company. But, thankfully, it now looked like the immediate future was going to be a lot brighter. Maybe.

1. This should read *chump*, but still!

2. Well, *bestest* until he finishes helping on the book, and then I'll go back to not talking to him.

The other half

Armed with *Old Scroat's*, we set about the task of predicting the rest of the 21st century. Suddenly things became so much easier; no more tiresome seances; no more throwing Scrabble letters and pretending they were runes. All we had to do now was copy stuff out of *Old Scroat's Almanac* and hope that Old Scroat never found out. What follows is the second half of the 21st century according to *Old Scroat's Almanac*, with additional advice from me and my team. So, we'll just down these pints of Sennapod Lager that Elderado very kindly brewed for us, and we'll get started. Oh – excuse me! That lager goes right through you!

The future is Scroat-shaped

Let's take the giant leap to the end of the century, stopping off every now and then to see what the future holds. For instance...

MONEY 2051-2100

Money will be as important in the second half of the 21st century as it ever was. Especially for those who haven't got any!

2054 will see the introduction of a whole new range of coins suitable for space travel. In order to combat weightlessness these will be very heavy. The 5p, for example, will weigh seven tonnes.

2077 The National Lottery will be cut back from 40 times a week to just 36, when a survey reveals the worrying fact that the Lottery causes people to buy lottery tickets.

2083 A precious ore will be discovered on another planet - possibly Jupiter. Because of its weight (very light) it will replace money. It'll also replace gold, supplies of which are running very low. The good news is that there will be endless supplies of this ore, to be named Wilbur, after the American astronaut who discovered it. The bad news is that it will look, smell and taste exactly like lemon sherbet. Maybe this is the *good* news! Unscrupulous people (i.e. virtually everybody) will be trying to pass sherbet off as Wilber - and succeeding. Because of this, sales of sherbet will be banned, causing a huge backlash from sherbetholics. These sad, addicted people will start eating their money (Wilber) instead, causing themselves to become penniless and homeless.

2091 The collapse of many world currencies will lead to a return to bartering. People will trade home-grown vegetables for pre-packed supermarket ones. This system will start to collapse when people realize that it costs two large turkeys to buy one small oven ready chicken.

TRAVEL 2051-2100

2067 A new breakthrough in space travel will be announced. No longer will it take nine months to fly to the Moon. Why? Because matter transfer will have been perfected. Sorry - perfected is not the right word. It'll be available if you want to take the risk. You've probably seen this on *Star Trek* and thought, "Wow! Wouldn't it be great to do that one day!" Well, now's your chance. But be warned: if you go with a friend you're likely to reach the other end wearing each other's clothes. This could break the ice if you're on a blind date, but otherwise it could just prove embarrassing.

2082 By now the parking problem is so bad that cars are actually designed to be parked on top of each other, but this will be solved virtually overnight. Well, it'll take six years, but that's virtually overnight when you consider how long the planet has been around. So how exactly will this miracle happen? Well, according to *Scroat's* it will be caused by the invention of the flying car.

People will naturally assume that because the car flies you will be able to park it absolutely anywhere, including up in the air. Brilliant! Everyone will rush out and buy one. They'll take it out for a spin, find the only available parking space, 25 metres off the ground, and then say, "How am I supposed to get out?" Another great idea will turn out to be a complete turkey; but two of these cars won't be worth an oven ready chicken.

THE THREE Rs 2051 - 2100

2055 Despite the technological advances, education will still be causing headaches. The worst thing is that – for all the technical advances – the exam results will seem to be taking a nose-dive. A committee will be set up to consider what to do.

2079 The committee will issue their first report. It will read: "We've run out of coffee."
2082 The committee will issue its second report. It will read: "It's OK – we'll have tea instead."
2094 The committee will issue its final report, which reads: "This is our final report. Can we have the cheque now please?[1]" Their report will make a number of radical suggestions. The main thrust of their argument

1. Cheques of course will no longer exist. They'll actually be given a huge bag of sherbet which will turn out to be counterfeit money.

will be that there's really no point in educating people, since computers are doing all the clever jobs anyway. Suddenly having a load of educational qualifications will be totally pointless, as well as uncool. GCSEs will be renamed Smartypants exams, and everyone will try to fail them. This will prove harder than you might think, mainly because exams will now be so easy that even a *teacher* could pass them.

COMMUNICATION 2051 - 2100

2054 The *Sun* newspaper, still going strong, will print a story that is totally unsensational and turns out to be completely true. Nobody will buy the paper that day.
2067 Communication by telepathy will be introduced. By developing a certain part of your brain you will be able to go into a shop and, without saying a word, buy anything. Unfortunately it won't be anything you want, because shop assistants won't have been able to develop the telepathic part of their brain, mainly because they haven't got one (a brain, that is)[1].
2087 The sun will be entirely obliterated from the Earth by the hundreds of communications satellites that have been launched since the first one in 1957. Fortunately, because most of them are made of shiny steel, they will reflect light and heat back on to the planet. They'll also keep the rain off.

1. Note to shop assistants: Only joking. If you understood it that is. If you didn't, I wasn't!

FASHION 2051-2100

Fashion will have to reflect the whole universe and not just Earth. Here's a quick trip through the half century, picking out some of fashion's finest moments.

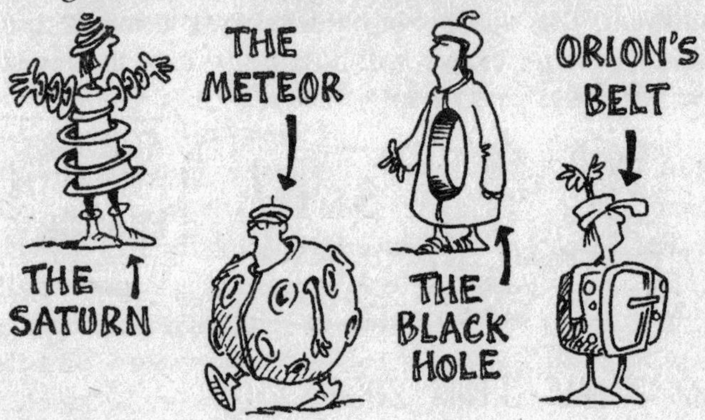

MEDICINE 2051-2100

In the early part of the mid-century there'll be a move by doctors to go back to the old methods of curing people. This will be due to a shortage of drugs, and the money (sorry – sherbet) to pay for them. Leeches will be used to cure blood disorders, as they had been for centuries before man started messing with nature. Other cures will include a badger on the head to cure earache, and a lion leaping out of a broom cupboard when you least expect it, to cure hiccups. The lion will also be used to remove unwanted limbs.

2067 Doctors will discover a way that we can all live for ever. This will come as good news to Thames Television, as they contemplate booking Cilla Black for another series of *Blind Date*. However, only the very stupid will think of taking advantage of eternal life. Anthea Turner will be first on the operating table.

LEISURE/SPORT 2051-2100

2060 The ball will be reintroduced in football, and the name will be changed back. Shortly after the rule change in the 2040s it was decided that the ball only got in the way. Also, it was regarded as potentially dangerous; suppose somebody tripped over it whilst carrying a broken bottle? So it was outlawed, and the game's name was changed to Foot, or more likely, Soc.

But by now Soc violence had become very sophisticated. It was no longer necessary to hit anyone. A sarcastic putdown, if said with the right sneer and toss of the head, could do more harm than the sub-machine-guns that had been so popular in the FA Cup replay of 2047 (when Ipswich fans won 2,345 to 43). But now that violence was verbal, there was no reason for the players to hide. After all, sneering wit couldn't possibly hurt them, because they wouldn't be able to understand it. They might as well come out on the field and well, kick a ball around. And so they will.

2066 Baby Spice will announce that she's to remarry her seventh husband, if she can remember who he was.

2075 Goalposts will be reintroduced into the game of football after it is realized that the players have nothing to kick the ball at, apart from each other – and that wouldn't be in the spirit of the game.

2089 Someone will score in a football match. The crowd will go wild and a fight will break out. The police will be forced to release wood pigeons skilled in the art of crowd control.

2097 Norway will win Eurovision. Belgium will demand a recount and this will almost cause a world war. Fortunately, veteran entertainer Bruce Forsyth, still going strong at the ripe old age of 169, will avert a global holocaust by threatening to tap-dance unless they all sit down and behave themselves.

EXPLORATION 2051-2100

2060 A second moon will be discovered. This will turn out to be the moon that appears in the sky during the day when the real moon has gone to bed. Up until now everyone has believed that they were one and the same moon. But Dr Herbacious Boarder, astrological scholar and chief shareholder in the *Trips To The Second Moon* travel company, will convince everyone that they are not. His forceful argument will be, "Why don't you buy a ticket and see for yourself?" He will become a Sherbet Millionaire overnight, and retire somewhere where nobody will ever find him.

2071 Huge deposits of gold will be found under a building in the city of London. It'll turn out to be the basement of the (now derelict) Bank of England.

LIFESTYLE 2051-2100

2062 A link is proved between coffee drinking and really bad singing. Coffee is banned in the backstage canteen of *Stars in their Eyes*.

2070 Scientists will develop the self-lighting cigarette. Early versions will have teething troubles; premature ignition will cause many smokers' trousers to be set on fire.

2099 Everyone the world over will gather just before midnight on 31 December to celebrate the end of the century and the beginning of a new one.

Party on!

As they stand there, clutching their styrofoam cup of Gannett's Mead, they'll wonder what the future holds, much as Ethelred did in AD 999.

Much as we're doing now. Except that we don't need to

wonder, do we? Because we've seen the future and it's ... well, it's *strange* to say the least. But if only half of the predictions that my team have unearthed come true, then it certainly won't be dull. So, as Mrs Wibley packs away her Scrabble tiles, Paddy O'Dors rolls up his astrological charts and hits the dog with them for no good reason; as Dave Dilks callously comments, "D'you know, accidentally eating Neville has given me quite an appetite!"; as Elderado offers us all one last rub-down with Futtock's Horse Liniment, and as Mickey Shorthouse passes round old school photos that he always assured me he'd destroyed, my team's work comes to an end.

Who can really tell what the 21st century holds? Certainly if Nostradamus is to be believed, the world will be over and done with by the year 2000. Perhaps the fact that a large number of computers fail to survive the Millennium Bug will cause people to rethink the future of computer technology and we'll become less dependent on them. Perhaps we won't. Perhaps we'll become more dependent on them. And then what?

Well, by the year 2030 computer experts predict that it will be possible to enter a complete virtual world. Imagine it: to the rest of your family you'll be sitting in front of your computer looking like a boiler repairman who's been attacked by 78 miles of electric cabling, waving your arms about, when in fact you'll be scuba-diving in a virtual coral sea, or leading a mutant army against the evil forces of Scag. Your entire world will consist of *now* - you won't need to worry about your homework, who's going to win Euro '36, or the 2038 World Cup - which by then will have been replaced with a spoon, making it easier to clean. You won't need to wash, tidy your room, feed your pet - nothing! Does that sound like bliss to you? Do you think that it sounds like the sort of thing that the average parent is going to let you get away with? Nor me!

The reality will be the 21st century, with you in it. Possibly *right* in it. Learning to cope. Somehow.

What am I saying, somehow? You've got this book! The product of painstaking research, astral exploring and a bit of clever guesswork. What more do you need? Printed between the pages of this tome is everything you'll need to get you through the 21st century. Armed with this small book, you'll be ready for whatever fate, or your mum, throws at you.

Answers to page 40:
How did you do?

1. Mirror (c1278)
2. Sequin (c1284)
3. Sewing machine (c1829)
4. Balaclava (c1855)
5. Leotard (c1895)
6. Artificial silk (c1884)
7. Zip (1893)
8. Nylon (1938)
9. Bikini (1946)
10. Velcro (1948)

Answers to page 46:
How did you do?

1. Electric battery invented (1800).
2. Toilet paper invented (1857). What did they do before then?
3. Chewing gum invented (1869).
4. Hi-fi system, originally called the gramophone (1888).
5. Latex rubber developed (1920).
6. Television invented (1926).
7. Penicillin discovered (1928).
8. Monopoly invented (1933).
9. FM radios developed (1933).
10. The first nylon toothbrush invented (1938).
11. M&Ms first appeared (1940).
12. Barbie was born (1959)!
13. England won the World Cup (1966).
14. Ray Dolby developed noise reduction for speakers (1967).